ELSTREE
CONFIDENTIAL

by

Paul Welsh MBE

Fifty Years of Studio Memories

PUBLISHED BY ELSTREE & BOREHAM WOOD MUSEUM

First published by

Elstree and Boreham Wood Museum in 2012

Published by Elstree and Boreham Wood Museum

1 Drayton Road, Borehamwood

Hertfordshire   WD6 2DA

www.elstree-museum.co.uk

email: office@elstree-museum.co.uk

ISBN 978-0-9565297-2-5

Subject categories APB, APFB, WQH (www.bic.org.uk)

Printed and bound in the UK by

MPG-Books Group, Bodmin and King's Lynn

01553 764728

Photography Credits and Copyright

Peter Beal	[© PB]
Rod Brewster	[© RB]
Captured Moments	[© CM]
Elstree and Boreham Wood Museum	[© EBWM]
First Impressions	[© FI]
Shirley-Anne Lord	[© SAL]
Ken Morris	[© KM]
Jonathan Sands	[© JS]
Paul Welsh	[© PW]

Contents

Foreword

The cinema and its stars have been a life-long interest to Paul Welsh. The tales he has to tell are centred on the district of Boreham Wood and Elstree, Hertfordshire, where he has lived and worked all his life.

The locality happens to be the home of famous Studios and the personalities he has written about are known the world over through the film and television industry generated in our town.

Without Paul's energies and influence during the 'Save Our Studios' campaign, Boreham Wood and Elstree would have lost their connection with this universal genre, which began here as long ago as 1914.

Happily, his first hand recollections of the international stars appearing in the locally made films are now captured for posterity in this book. Along with Elstree generated celluloid, they have a deserved place in the history of our town.

ELSTREE & BOREHAM WOOD MUSEUM

Preface

This book is my chance to share some of my memories of film and television personalities whom I met over fifty years. I apologise now if it appears to be one long name dropping exercise. I can make no excuses as that is what it is, but then what else can it be if I am to recall meetings with those who inhabit the film and television world?.

The two things of which I am most proud in life both revolve around Elstree Studios.

The first is having chaired the Save Our Studios campaign which lasted an amazing 8 years from 1988 to 1996 and now to see a successful studio thriving today.

The second is being awarded the MBE in 1997, which stands for the Most Excellent Order of the British Empire and not more brown envelopes as some of my friends would have you believe. To my knowledge, I was only the second person to be so recognised in the history of Elstree Studios, the other being the late Andrew Mitchell who was managing director for many years.

I must thank the photographers who, over the years, managed to capture some of my star encounters especially at the Plaque unveilings and film evenings. The list includes Ken Morris who has been a good friend along with his wife Wendy, Peter Beal and Rod Brewster plus the team at Captured Moments. I am forever grateful as there is nothing like an old photo to jog a memory. Sadly, on many occasions when I interviewed stars, I felt it unprofessional to ask them to pose for a photo with me, which I now really regret as I doubt they would have minded.

Then there was Jonathan Sands, another good mate, who ran the Elstree stills department for several years and is now Chief Executive of the excellent London Film Museum.

You can imagine over 50 years I have collected many, many photos. Some taken by myself, some given to me. Except for those taken by the mates I have just named and by my own efforts I believe the rest are copyright orphans given to me over the decades.

I thank MGM, Warner Bros, Universal, Paramount, Hammer, 20th Century Fox, Sony Columbia, Lucas Film and others who made so many of the films at Elstree, the sets of which I was privileged to visit.

Finally, thanks to my friends at Elstree and Boreham Wood Museum who enabled this book to be published, including David Taylor for editing and design, and the team of proof-readers.

We have called this book, *Elstree Confidential,* but don't expect scandal and gossip. The material is drawn from my private archives and personal memories. Most of the content has not previously appeared in other publications, so hopefully will interest readers.

Paul Welsh MBE

Behind the Scenes

A tribute to the thousands of people, sometimes whole families, who worked in the Boreham Wood Studios and enabled talented actors to become stars and who cannot all be mentioned individually.

A Brief History of the Studios

The story of Borehamwood's film making past goes back nearly a century to 1914 when the area was little more than a rural village surrounded by farms and open land.

The Neptune Studios Site

In 1914 pioneer film producers Percy Nash and John East spotted the potential of the area. It was close to London, served by a rail link opened in 1868, the Great North Road and Watling Street, and it was free of the smog belt that often engulfed the metropolis. It also boasted a variety of local locations within easy reach. Land could be purchased for £100 an acre.

They built *Neptune Studios* which was billed as having one of the first *dark* stages in the UK lit by electricity from generators rather than relying on a glass roof to provide natural light.

In those days films were silent and cinema was dominated by Hollywood movies featuring stars such as *Charlie Chaplin, Mary Pickford* and *Douglas Fairbanks*. It is ironic that both *Charlie* and *Mary* were to visit Borehamwood in the 1930s and in the same decade *Douglas Faibanks* was to make his last ever movie here.

This first studio went into liquidation in 1917, and became *Ideal Studios* within a couple of years. Within the next two decades it became known as *Blattner, Rock* and then *British National* under the ownership of *Lady Yule*. Home grown British stars such as *George Formby, Old Mother Riley, Bud Flannagan* and even *Bill Owen* made films at the studio.

In the early 1950s *Douglas Fairbanks Jr* leased the facility to produce television films with film production continuing to the end of the decade. TV series shot at *National* by various companies included *"The Invisible Man"* and *"William Tell"*.

ATV purchased the site and at the beginning of the 1960s converted it for television production and went on to produce thousands of programmes the most successful of which was *"The Muppet Show"*.

In 1984 the *BBC* acquired the facility and renamed it the *BBC Elstree Centre* and in subsequent years have produced such programmes as *"Top Of The Pops"*, *"Grange Hill"*, *"Holby City"* and of course it is home to *"EastEnders"* which nowadays dominates the site.

The British International Pictures Site

In 1925 more film pioneers set their sights on Borehamwood and this time they purchased 40 acres of land on the opposite side of the road and built what is known today as *Elstree Studios*. In the pre war days it was known as *British International Pictures* and after the war until 1969 as *Associated British Picture Corporation.*

1920s productions at the facility included the first British talkie *"Blackmail"* directed by a young *Alfred Hitchcock* and *"Atlantic"* which was the first film shot in three languages.

The studio was closed during the war years and requisitioned by the government for storage and as a garrison theatre. By the end of the 1940s *ABPC*, with investment from *Warner Bros*, was extensively rebuilt and reopened with the production of such films as *"The Hasty Heart"* starring *Richard Todd* and future *USA President, Ronald Reagan,* and *"Stage Fright"* starring *Marlene Dietrich.*

The 1950s saw the filming of movies such as *"The Dam Busters"* and *"Moby Dick"* with the 1960s bringing *"The Rebel"* and *"Summer Holiday".*

ABPC was taken over by *EMI* in 1969 and they continued to own it until 1986. During that period it went through some rocky times, but continued to be the home of such films as *"Murder On The Orient Express"*, *"Raiders of The Lost Ark"*, *"Star Wars"* and *"Julia".*

In 1986 the studio was sold to *Cannon* who ran into financial difficulties and they sold it in 1988 to *Brent Walker.* The subsequent history is related in this book. The studio continues to thrive today.

British and Dominions Imperial Studios

Alongside *B.I.P.*, where *Imperial Place* office complex now stands, was constructed a purpose built sound studio in the late 1920s called *British*

& *Dominions Imperial Studios*. It was here in 1933 that *Alexander Korda* made *"The Private Life of Henry VIII"* which won *Charles Laughton* an Oscar and launched a boom in British film investment. Sadly the studio was destroyed by fire in 1936.

Danzigers' New Elstree Studio

Rivalling for the record of the shortest-lived studio in the area must be the *Danzigers' New Elstree Studio* which actually was located in *Elstree* unlike the rest that were *Borehamwood* based. It lasted only about 6 years from the mid 1950s, but during that period produced hundreds of B movies and TV series, which employed many a grateful technician and actor. The studio was also used by outside companies such as *Hammer* who made *"Quatermass II"* there. The studio was demolished to make way for a business park.

The Gate Studio

The *Gate Studio*, situated by the railway station, was opened as a silent stage in 1928 and was then known as the *Whitehall Studio*. Within two years of opening it was hastily converted to service sound movies, but its proximity to the railway compromised its use. However, feature films including an early movie starring *Cary Grant* and *"Odette"* starring *Anna Neagle* continued to be produced there until the 1950s, including religious films for *J Arthur Rank*, before it became a cinema screen factory. The barely altered facility remained until demolished a few years ago.

Metro Goldwyn Mayer

Perhaps the Rolls Royce of film studios was *MGM* that occupied 115 acres of land alongside *Elstree Way*. A brief history of this marvellous facility is given in this book.

Millennium Studios

We must also mention the converted buildings opposite the former *MGM* site which in the 1990s opened as the *Millennium Studios* and played host to a number of productions and provided a safe haven for several companies who were displaced when *Elstree Studios* was closed between 1993 to 1996.

Overall, *Elstree & Borehamwood* have probably played host to more television and film productions than anywhere outside of *Los Angeles*. From *Buster Keaton* to the *Beatles*, from *Alfred Hitchcock* to *Steven Spielberg* and from *Clark Gable* to *Harrison Ford*, they have all been driven along *Shenley Road* at some time, which is quite something for a small town in Hertfordshire.

Sylvia Syms and John Mills
in
'Ice Cold in Alex'

A banner promoting
Elstree's Screen Heritage

Filming at Elstree in 1930. Note the camera and operator confined to a sound proof box to prevent noise.
[© PW]

The first sound stage at Elstree Studios in the 1920s with a young Alfred Hitchcock
and stars of various films in production [© PW]

The fire that destroyed the British and Dominions Studios [© EBWM]

The Elstree Studios Fire Brigade led by Studio Manager Joe Grossman
who attended the fire that destroyed the adjoining British and Dominion Studios in 1936. [© PW]

My First Autograph

Back in November 1960 my late father, Bill, who worked at the Gate Recording Theatre in Borehamwood, suggested I might like to pop down to the adjacent *Elstree Film Studios* to get the autograph of an old Hollywood star. It was to be my first visit to this world famous dream factory.

The actor was *Gary Cooper* who was shooting his final movie *"The Naked Edge"* just prior to his death from cancer. He seemed a gentleman and quite reserved, but many years later I learnt from other actors in the film such as *Peter Cushing* and *Deborah Kerr* that he was in some pain from his illness and the English winter was doing him no favours. Although Gary became an American icon and the epitome of the western star, his parents were actually English and for several years he was sent back from their home in America to be educated in Dunstable – a fact commemorated by the naming of a pub in that town after him.

Gary Cooper

Gary Cooper on location in London meets a local fireman [© PW]

Deborah Kerr told me that she only took the role in the film in order to work with the great man and *Peter Cushing* recalled that he had grown up watching *Gary* on screen so was overawed to meet him.

The late great director *Fred Zinnemann* who directed *Gary Cooper* in his best remembered movie, the classic *"High Noon"* told me *'The thing about Coop was that when you watched him on set acting you felt he was hardly giving a performance and was just walking through the part. However, the next day when you watched the rushes he just lit up the screen. It was certainly a case of the camera loving him. He never felt he was a great actor but he just had that extra something that the cinemagoers adored."*

So you could say that I started at the top with my star encounters but as that young kid I never dreamt those encounters would continue for another 50 years and have still not stopped!

Deborah Kerr

Signed photo of Deborah Kerr [© PW]

Hollywood

David Niven

David Niven was certainly old-school Hollywood and my chance to meet him was in 1979 when he came to *Elstree Studios* to make a television film called *"A Man Called Intrepid"*.

I went down to the set and there was *David* filming a scene with *Michael York* in which he sat behind a desk examining top secret papers as *David* was portraying a spymaster in the Second World War. After the scene was shot I took the opportunity to look at the secret files and they turned out to be not so secret transport dockets from the Bullens Removals firm that was based next door to the studio.

I was surprised how nervous *David* seemed filming a scene and afterwards he told me *"It never seems to get easier and my palms sweat even doing chat show interviews."*

I asked about his two best selling books *"The Moon's A Balloon"* and *"Bring On The Empty Horses"* wearing my historian's hat and *David* confided *"I set out to write an amusing story of my life, but let's say from a historical point of view it is not entirely accurate."* In fact other actors later told me that he had pinched anecdotes of things that had happened to them and put them into his own story. Perhaps that is why he always declined being the subject of the *"This Is Your Life"* TV programme.

David Niven relaxes while filming. [© PW]

Patricia Dainton, Caesar Romero, Vera Ellen, Richard Todd, Diane Hart and David Niven all filming at Elstree, drafted in to attend a charity event in the 1950s. [© PW]

David had arrived in Hollywood in the early 1930s and gained quite a reputation as a ladies' man which no doubt helped his climb to stardom. For a while he shared a house with the legendary **Errol Flynn** which they nicknamed *"Cirrhocis by the Sea"*. He told me that Errol was a great charmer but totally unreliable and seemed hell bent on enjoying life to the full, saying that your first 50 years are all that matter. Ironically, Errol died aged 50 with a body ravaged by various illnesses plus drink and drugs.

David was very popular with film crews and fellow cast members and came across as a real gent. Perhaps it was the tragedy of his life that his first wife, whom he adored, died tragically young when she fell down a flight of stairs during a Hollywood party game of hide and seek. Equally sad were the last years of his life when he was struck by motor neurone disease and his wife of that time, an alcoholic, seemed to care little for him.

He was a realist as he confided with me, *"Many of my films were crap and some I made just for the money. Whenever I had a decent movie like "Separate Tables" it never seemed to lead to other good roles so the length of my career has surprised even me."*

David's death in 1983 put an end to a great career.

Bob Hope

On three occasions I have travelled the 6,000 miles to the Mecca of film production which is, of course, Hollywood.

Each time I stayed at the historic Roosevelt Hotel where the first *Oscar* ceremony took place. It is ideally situated on Hollywood Boulevard, and opposite the Chinese Theatre where you can see the hand prints of Tinseltown's great film stars dating back to the 1920s.

Naturally, star encounters came with the territory and the biggest was the legendary *Bob Hope.* He was visiting the hotel to publicise the annual Christmas parade and the Mayor of Hollywood invited me to meet the great man.

It was my pleasure and I was equally pleased when it was suggested that we posed for a photo together. At that moment a group of British tourists joined us so it became a group shot with Bob standing on a dais above me but with his hand resting on my shoulder for balance.

He quipped *"What's happened? Have you all been deported?"*.

Bob Hope, the Mayor of Hollywood and me, standing just below for what was meant to be a nice shot of the three of us until my fan club heard I was in Hollywood – the price of fame. [© PW]

Mae Clarke

On another visit I was invited to a Gangsters' and Molls' Celebrity party and we all had to dress accordingly. I wore a mafia-style outfit of a suit, black shirt and white tie. It was a great evening full of stars of yesteryear and I got to sit next to *Mae Clarke* who had starred with *Boris Karloff* in the first *"Frankenstein"* movie and had a grapefruit quashed into her face by *James Cagney* in *"Public Enemy"*. In the early hours having consumed one or ten drinks I decided to go for a walk along what was then a rather seedy Hollywood Boulevard. Not far from the hotel a police car pulled up and asked me if I was lost, albeit dressed as a mafia hood.

When they heard my limey accent, they jokingly said *"We don't recommend even the Mafia wander these streets at night, Sir"*.

Andrew Mitchell, the late great Managing Director of Elstree Studios, had written me a letter of introduction so I got to be given personal tours of *Warner Bros, 20th Century Fox, Universal, Paramount and MGM,* which for me was just overwhelming.

Mae Clarke
who appeared with
James Cagney
in Public Enemy
[© PW]

Signed note from 1930s
Hollywood star
Mae Clarke in 1988
when I sat next to her at a
'Gangsters' and Molls' Evening
in Hollywood
[© PW]

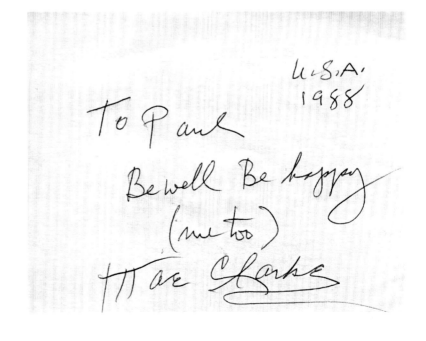

At *Warner Brosthers'* I got to see *James Dean's* motorbike and the piano from *"Casablanca"*, met *Tony Curtis* in the car park, visited the set of *"The Waltons"* and had a chat with *Ralph Waite*. At *20ᵗʰ Century Fox,* on different visits, I went on the set of *"Die Hard"* and *"X Files The Movie'"* On the latter they asked me to sign a form I would never reveal anything I saw being filmed. I told them it was only a movie and not to be silly.

At *Paramount* I met *Michael J Fox* on the set of the TV series *"Family Ties"* and stood by the famous gate arch entrance.

At *MGM* I got to stand on the sound stages where so many great films were shot and on the restaurant steps on the exact spot that *Katie Hepburn* met *Spencer Tracy* for the first time.

Apparently, they were about to make their first film together and *Katie* said *"I hope I am not too tall for you, Mr Tracy"* to which he replied *"Don't worry I will cut you down to size, Miss Hepburn."*

On a side visit to Las Vegas I had been privileged to meet *MGM* star *Debbie Reynolds* and saw some of the wonderful costumes she had purchased from the studio and which were recently sold for a fortune.

At *Universal* a nice lady was assigned to show me around but made the mistake of suggesting we partake first in some Californian wine and as you know one bottle is never enough. We eventually set off a bit tipsy in one of those studio "golf carts" and dangerously navigated various sets on the backlot ending up at the *Bates Motel* which featured in *"Psycho"*.

I stood at the door of the house, once occupied by *Tony Perkins* as the psycho killer, looking a bit worse for wear when a trolley full of Japanese tourists drove slowly past snapping away with their cameras. Over 20 years later they, no doubt, pull out their family albums of holiday snaps and point me out as *Norman Bates* returned!

Alcohol featured in another sad incident at the hotel, when I was asked to join a panel of people judging how funny a pilot episode of a comedy series was, featuring *Faye Dunaway*.

The sun had passed the yard arm and I had imbibed a few drinks, so when they gave me an electronic box to register, via various coloured buttons, how funny I thought each sentence uttered was, it was a touch confusing. I think I must have pressed the unfunny button too many times, but I hope that was not the only reason the show never went on air!

Debbie Reynolds

Signed photo of Debbie Reynolds. We met in Las Vegas. [© PW]

Resting Places

I could not resist paying my respects to the Hollywood greats no longer with us, so that meant visiting various cemeteries. It seemed odd that **Bela Lugosi**, who was buried in his *"Dracula"* cape, was interred just yards away from **Bing Crosby** although they died 20 years apart.

Al Jolson's memorial contained a life-size statue and a cascading waterfall, ensuring it could be seen from a nearby highway.

Rudolph Valentino was interred in a wall crypt in a vast mausoleum. Just across from him was **Peter Finch**, who the attendant told me had originally been buried outside, but his family later decided he would prefer to be indoors!

I arrived at the Jewish cemetery only an hour before it closed and the gravediggers looked on in amusement as I ran around ticking off the graves of **Jack Benny, Jeff Chandler, Michael Landon** and **Eddie Cantor**. Luckily, being English out in the midday sun, saved me from being sent off to an asylum.

Al Jolson

Longshot of Al Jolson's modest tomb in Los Angeles complete with waterfall. [© PW]

Closeup of Al Jolson's tomb with life-sized statue of the great man. Gives me an idea for mine. [© PW]

Liberace

Liberace now resides here. [© PW]

Bette Davis

Bette Davis's final resting place. [© PW]

It was moving to stand next to the outdoor wall crypt containing the legendary *Marilyn Monroe*. Other stars I visited included *Rita Hayworth, Sharon Tate, Buster Keaton, George Raft*, and *Laurel and Hardy*

Stars at Elstree

Vincent Price

Vincent Price. [© PW]

In the good old days films used to solicit publicity during production to help build up interest when that were released, but now the common policy is to have closed sets.

I was lucky to have been around when things were easier and a good example was the Amicus movie *"The Monster Club"* shot at *Elstree* in 1980.

I phoned the producer *Milton Subotsky* to ask if I could visit the set and do some interviews and he answered *"Yes"* so off I went. The unit publicist mentioned the film was costing less than one million pounds, but *Milton* chipped in saying *"There are more dollars than pounds so describe it as a multi-million dollar production which sounds better!"*

I asked *"Who can I interview?"* and the answer was *"Anybody I wished"* so over the next two days I met *Vincent Price, John Carradine, Britt Ekland, Richard Johnson, Anthony Valentine and Donald Pleasance.*

I recall talking to *Donald* about the film *"Dr Crippen"* he had starred in at the studio in the early 1960s. He told me his hobby, at that time, had been going to watch real trials at the Old Bailey. Donald had an amazing career but I must admit I can't say I warmed to him as a person.

Vincent Price was looking frailer than I had remembered him in all those great horror movies of the 1950s and 1960s, but was every inch a gentleman. He had a huge knowledge of art and cooking, as wells a delightful sense of humour. I recalled that on an earlier visit to *Elstree* to make *"Dr Phibes"* he had been photographed mailing his Oscar nomination papers in the post box at the top of Eldon Avenue opposite the studio. It had amused him that nobody took any notice of the king of horror in their vicinity.

Poor old *John Carradine* seemed a bit out of it at this stage of his life and it was sad to notice both his hands severely crippled with arthritis.

I wish now I had taped the conversations, as all these actors had wonderful memories and enjoyed lengthy careers.

Dermot O'Leary is best known nowadays as the host of *"X Factor"*, but a few years ago when he was involved with *"Big Brother"*, he also had his own production company and decided to make a TV documentary on being a fan of *"Star Wars"*.

Dave Prowse MBE

"Darth Vader", alias my old friend *Dave Prowse* and myself were invited to participate in Dermot's Documentary. For some reason *Dermot*, as the on screen host, was dressed as *"Luke Skywalker"*, but without trousers which no doubt was appreciated by the female viewers. It was fun to do and *Dermot* was friendly, polite and a nice guy.

It is always a pleasure to meet *Dave* who travels the world attending *"Star Wars"* events, even though *Lucas Film* appear not to be that happy with him. *Dave* was equally hurt when they not only dubbed his character in the films, which was understandable due to his accent, but used another actor's face when he was finally demasked on screen.

Dave also appeared as the *"Frankenstein"* monster at Elstree in a *Hammer* film and was famous as the TV safety advert's *"Green Cross Code Man"*, all of which contributed to him being awarded an *MBE*. Sadly in recent years ill health has presented significant challenges for him, but never kept him down. He raises a great deal of money for charity and he is certainly a gentle giant.

Dave 'Darth Vader' Prowse. [© KM]

Douglas Fairbanks Jr. KBE

A name from the golden age of Hollywood must surely be **Douglas Fairbanks Jr**, whose father was the king of Tinseltown in the silent era and his stepmother **Mary Pickford** was America's screen sweetheart.

I first met **Doug** in 1984 when he accepted an invite to attend the first *"Elstree Film Evening"* at the studio along with **Dame Anna Neagle** returning to her film home for the last time before her death in 1986.

Douglas Fairbanks Jr and Dame Anna Neagle at Elstree Studios in 1984. [© PW]

Douglas Fairbanks Senior and Junior strolling in London
during filming in Borehamwood in the 1930s. [© PW]

Doug was every inch a Hollywood star, still upright and good looking in old age. His career had included such swashbuckling films as *"The Prisoner Of Zenda"* and after a highly decorated and distinguished war career was knighted for his services to Anglo-American relations.

We had lunch at the studio hosted by the managing director *Andrew Mitchell* and our fellow guests included Titanic survivor *Eva Hart* and the then *Lord Lieutenant of Hertfordshire Major General Sir George Burns*, former A.D.C. to the last *Viceroy of India.* It was a memorable meal listening to these fascinating people, all of whom are sadly no longer with us.

Doug accepted my invite to visit twice again in the 1980s. On one occasion I escorted him to the *BBC Elstree Centre* where in the 1950s he had produced 160 made-for-television programmes. They had agreed to name the admin. building

after him and he duly cut the ribbon with a sword stroke to the flash of news photographers' cameras. We then went for a tour which included dropping in on the *"Queen Vic pub"* on the *"EastEnders"* set, which brought filming to a halt. I had a brief chat with *"Dirty Den"* alias actor *Leslie Grantham* and I remember as we were leaving, *Nick Berry* and *Gillian Taylforth* ran after him for an autograph. *Nick* went on to further success in *"Heartbeat"* and *Gillian* in *"Footballers' Wives".*

Doug was always good fun and in 1989 he kindly invited me to visit him in his New York penthouse.

The previous year, I had visited his father's elaborate tomb in the *"Hollywood Forever Cemetery".* When *Doug* died he was buried with his father.

Douglas Fairbanks Jr. [© PW]

Douglas Fairbanks Jr unveiling the offices named after him
at the BBC Elstree Centre. [© PW]

Anthony Quinn

In the early 1990s I heard a rich American heiress
was staging a night of 100 stars in aid of charity
in London's West End and I eagerly booked my
front row seat to enjoy a once in a lifetime feast of
nostalgia. The cabaret was performed by **Michael
Bolton, Petula Clark and David Cassidy,** but
for me the thrill was to be able to shake hands
with a wealth of old time Hollywood stars. They
included **Ginger Rogers, Van Johnson, Esther
Williams, Robert Wagner, Roddy McDowall**
to name a few. I ended up showing **Gene Barry**
and **Cliff Robertson** to their seats as the young
usherettes did not recognise the old stars and left
them to struggle in the darkness.

I also met **Anthony Quinn.** I had previously
encountered him at **Elstree Studios** when he was
filming **"The Greek Tycoon"**. On that occasion
he asked if there was a local bookshop and we
walked down Shenley Road to the one that used
to front the **Borehamwood Times**. The purpose
was to buy copies of his autobiography to give to
visiting journalists that afternoon! As a thank
you he signed a 10x 8 photo for me and inscribed
it **"Keep smiling"**, as he thought I looked too
serious.

Signed photo of Anthony Quinn,
given to me while he was at Elstree Studios
starring in 'The Greek Tycoon'. [© PW]

Mark Hamill

Mark Hamill shot to fame in the 1970s as the young hero *"Luke Skywalker"* in the original *"Star Wars Trilogy"* shot at *Elstree Studios*. By the time they came to film the third instalment, then known as *"Revenge Of The Jedi"* but released as *"Return Of The Jedi"*, *Mark* was world famous.

I had been arranging and hosting *"Meet a Star Evenings"* at the local *Maxwell Youth Centre* to encourage youngsters to attend the facility. We had already staged events with boxing champ *Alan Minter, Spurs* footballer *Glenn Hoddle*, Arsenal player *Graham Rix*, Blue Peter presenter *Peter Duncan* and the then *"Dr Who" Peter Davison.* I chanced my luck and asked *Mark* if he would be willing to be a guest, perhaps sparing an hour after filming. He readily agreed, but when we arrived, the Centre was jam-packed full of 300 eager youngsters. By the time he had answered questions and signed autographs at least twice the allotted time had passed. I worried that *Mark* would be upset as he had an early call the next morning, but a couple of days later a handwritten letter arrived saying how much he had enjoyed meeting the kids and how it had put him back in touch with the audience, for whom they were making the movies, which I thought was a nice gesture from a nice guy.

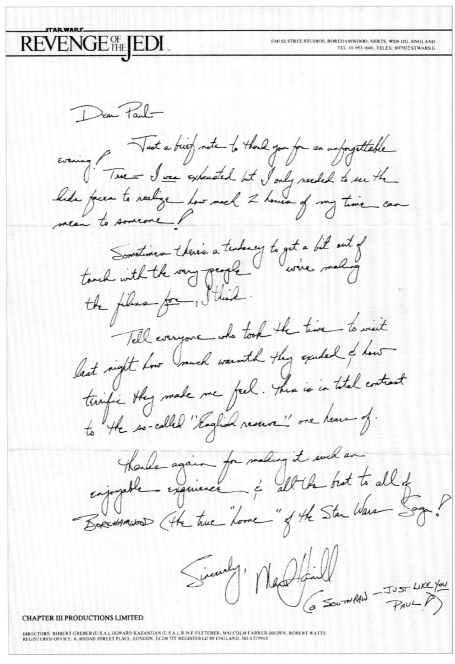

Letter from Mark Hamill thanking me after he had attended
an event for youngsters at Maxwell Youth Centre in the early 1980s

Andrew Lancel

Among my younger, or should I now say youngish, friends in the acting profession is Andrew Lancel.

I joke with him that he owes his success to my inviting him to one of our Elstree Film Evenings in the mid 1990s. In fact, Andrew had just enjoyed success playing a doctor in a TV series called *"Cardiac Arrest"*. Later, he went on to spend several years portraying a police detective in the hit TV series *"The Bill"* and, at the time of writing, is the latest villain in *"Coronation Street"*.

'The Bill' star Andrew Lancel. [© CM]

In 2007 Andrew invited me to join him at a posh awards dinner at a top London hotel. It was a black tie job and I was a bit reluctant to go, but he insisted. When I arrived we sat at a table occupied by other cast members of *"The Bill"* and next to me was actor and singer *Jess Conrad,* who looked little different from when he was the face of 1960. *Jess* made several films in Borehamwood and was a pin up boy in the swinging 60s. He still performs in those nostalgia music concerts and is a fun person to know.

Andrew was called up on stage to present the *"Film Heritage Award"* and I suddenly realised I was to be the recipient! After some very kind words, I was asked on stage where compere *Bobby Davro* handed me the award and there was a standing ovation. It is immodest to tell this story, but once again I was very proud, because it was for my long term efforts to preserve and publicise our *Elstree Film Heritage* and it showed other people cared. I did not spend 8 years fighting to save Elstree motivated by or thinking I would end up with awards, but they were much appreciated. The wine certainly flowed that night.

I don't want to give the impression I am always drinking. I know my doctor sometimes worries about my alcohol consumption, so I told him I had gone 28 days without a drink. He seemed so pleased, I did not have the heart to tell him that was spread over 40 years. When he advised me to be a sensible drinker, I assumed that meant get other people to buy the rounds – Boom, Boom!.

My Heritage Award presentation by Andrew Lancel and Bobby Davro. [© PW].

Liz Fraser

Liz Fraser is a national treasure having made film and TV appearances with every major comedy star you can think of. She also starred in several of the early *"Carry On"* movies. She is a fine actress and has enjoyed a long and successful career. *Liz* is also a feisty lady and holds strong opinions, which is great and is certainly not the scatty character she sometimes portrays on screen.

Liz was also a strong supporter of the *"Elstree Film Evenings"* I organised and I was always grateful for her support. I remember walking through the Borehamwood street market with *Liz* and her beloved dog, although I can't remember why we were there. I can't wait to read her autobiography. She is truly one of the comedy greats.

Liz Fraser. [© CM]

Sir Nigel Hawthorne and Liz Fraser at the re opening of Elstree Studios in 1996. [© CM]

Peggy Cummins

Another lovely lady and good supporter of my events is *Peggy Cummins,* who starred in many films from the 1940s onwards. She was the co-star of a marvellous supernatural thriller shot at *Elstree* called *"Night Of The Demon"*.

It was made in 1956/7 and starred *Dana Andrews,* who, sadly at this point in his career, was suffering severe drinking problems. The producer, *Hal Chester,* told me he knew he had problems when *Dana* flew in from *Hollywood* and fell down the aircraft steps.

The film was a low budget horror movie, but was so well made it has become a cult classic around the world. In 1987 I requested we showed this old black and white movie to the teenagers of the then *"Elstree Youth Theatre"* at the studio.

The powers to be thought it was a poor selection for showing to kids who had grown up on colour slasher films, which were far more graphic. It turned out *"Night Of The Demon"* still gave the audience shocks and they enjoyed it.

Twenty plus years later *Peggy* joined us at the *"Elstree Film Festival"* at our local cinema and, after we did an interview in front of the audience, I joined her to watch the film which she had not seen for many years.

Peggy spoke warmly of *Dana,* who later beat his alcohol problem and lived a long life. *Peggy* is a charming lady and lovely company.

Peggy Cummins. [© CM]

Peter Cushing OBE

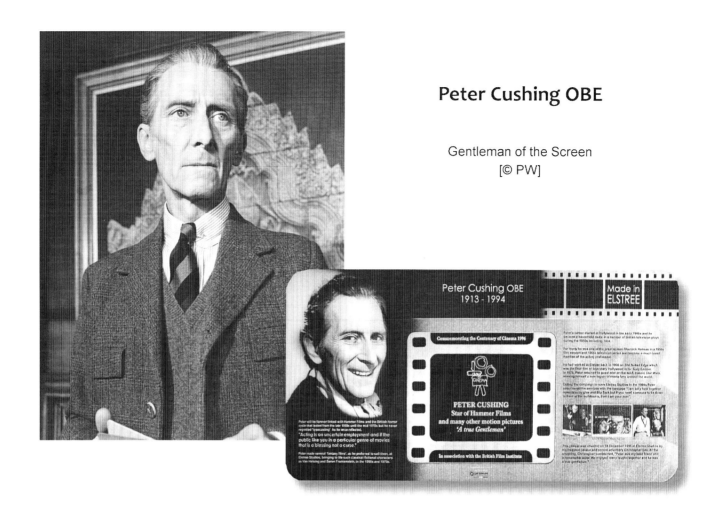

Gentleman of the Screen
[© PW]

Peter Cushing OBE
1913 - 1994

Made in ELSTREE

Commemorating the Centenary of Cinema 1996

PETER CUSHING
Star of Hammer Films
and many other motion pictures
'A true Gentleman'

In association with the British Film Institute

My first real interview, complete with tape recorder was in 1973 with *Peter Cushing* at *Shepperton Studio* on the set of *"The Beast Must Die"*, and, by the way, the film certainly did. Sadly, *Peter* had lost his beloved wife a couple of years earlier and had lost interest in life. He looked forward to the day he could join her. However, he was kind and considerate to this, then, young writer and we chatted about his career and how he started in Hollywood after his dad paid for a one way ticket to Tinseltown.

Within a couple of years, he had co-starred with *Carol Lombard*, acted with *Laurel and Hardy* and was a long term house guest of *Ida Lupino*. However, he became homesick and eventually worked his way home, where in the early 1950s he became a big TV star on the *BBC*. He went to *Hammer* to play *"Sherlock Holmes"*, *"Van Helsing"* and *"Baron Frankenstein"* and the rest is movie history. *Peter* was a chain smoker, but I noticed he wore a white glove. He told me it was to prevent nicotine stains on his fingers which might offend some viewers in closeup scenes.

Three years later he was at *Elstree* guest starring in *"Star Wars"*. He said *"I am not really a fan of science fiction, but I am a fan of working! I was given what seemed to me like an Edwardian chauffeur's costume and my character's name sounded like 'grand moth'. Young George Lucas is a fine director"*

Later I heard that his costume's knee-length boots were a bad fit and whenever possible he asked to be shot from waist high, so he was actually commanding the death star in comfy carpet slippers.

In the early 1990s when *Elstree* was closed and things looked pretty bleak, *Peter* was quite frail and suffering from cancer. He sent me a letter saying *"Dear Paul, I am held together by blue tack and string, but if you need me to join you in front of the bulldozers, I will be there"*.

When he died, the streets of his beloved Whitstable were lined by hundreds of residents for the funeral, knowing he was finally able to join his dear wife Helen. At his request, their grave would be unmarked so they could rest in peace. In 1996 I invited his co-star of many films, *Sir Christopher Lee,* to unveil a Plaque in his honour at the Studios. We all agreed *Peter* had been a true gentleman, loved by film crews and fellow actors alike.

The England World Cup Football Team of 1982

Although not film or television stars, I must tell you about meeting the *England World Cup Football Squad of 1982,* just to show I sometimes mix with fellow athletes.

I decided to run a competition for Borehamwood youngsters to increase attendance at *Maxwell Youth Club* and wrote to the *England Manager, Ron Greenwood,* to ask if we might come to the training ground. Life was much simpler then and such requests were sometimes granted. *Ron* replied saying *"Yes",* but suggested we came to their hotel near Barnet instead, where the atmosphere was more relaxed and the players more accessible. This proved to be true and we mixed and mingled with the cream of football.

At the end, *Ron* met us in the lobby and asked if everybody had enjoyed themselves. One kid replied saying they had not met *Kevin Keegan*!

Ron asked the trainer where he was and the answer was that *Kevin* was resting in his room. *Ron* picked up the phone, spoke to him saying a group of youngsters were keen to meet him and I was told to take them up to his bedroom.

Although unwell and in bed, *Kevin* kindly signed autographs and posed for a souvenir photo. Can you imagine getting that level of support today or that access?. It was a memorable, once in a lifetime, day for those kids, who must now be in their 40s, and, no doubt, some with kids of their own.

Local Borehamwood kids meeting the England World Cup Squad in 1982. [© PW]

Kevin Keegan welcomes members of the Maxwell Park Youth Club. [© PW]

Elstree Confidential

More autographs from the England World Cup Squad in 1982. [© PW]

John Wayne

John Wayne on the set of 'Brannigan'. [PW]

John Wayne visited Borehamwood to guest star in a *Glen Campbell* music special at *ATV.* I got to meet the legendary Hollywood star in London on the set of a film called *"Brannigan"*, which was originally entitled *"Joe Battle"* but, apparently, thought the title sounded too violent.

We had a brief chat and my memory of him was a very sore sounding cough and a slightly ill-fitting toupee. Of course, the Duke was not the only star to wear a hairpiece. Other hair-challenged actors included *Fred Astaire, Bing Crosby, Gary Cooper* and *Ray Milland*.

He did impart a pearl of wisdom to me with regard to the career path of all actors. He said *"They start by saying "Who is John Wayne? Then you hit success and it becomes "We must have John Wayne". After a period of time, as you age, it turns to "We must have a John Wayne type" and if you live long enough it returns to "Who is John Wayne?"*

The Duke enjoyed a 50 year run of stardom in Hollywood, but in the 1970s he was struck down with the return of cancer that had robbed him of one lung ten years earlier in the 1960s. I can never forget seeing his last appearance on TV in a telecast of the Oscar ceremony, in which he presented an award. He walked on to a standing ovation, but everyone could see how frail and thin he looked, even though he was apparently wearing padding under his clothes. The Duke commented that he had arrived in Hollywood in 1928, the same year as the Academy Award *Oscar* and aimed to be around a whole lot longer. Sadly, within months he was dead and, I am told was originally buried in an unmarked grave to deter it becoming a tourist haunt.

There was another Hollywood and music legend I did get to meet at *ATV* in *Borehamwood* and that was *Bing Crosby.* He came to the studio to film his annual Christmas special, even though it was taped in mid summer. The supporting cast included *David Bowie*, with whom he sang a duet and comedy star *Stanley Baxter.*

I believe it might have been the last time *Bing* sang *"White Christmas"* on camera, which must be the best selling record of all time. After his death, a couple of months later from a heart attack on a golf course in Spain, much was written about him and not all good. Unlike his passive, likeable screen image, it was said he had been an alcoholic early in his career and used to beat his sons, some of whom had tragic ends. Whatever the truth, *Bing* was one of the best selling recording artistes of the 20th century. I saluted his grave when I visited it in Los Angeles.

Stanley Baxter at Barbara Windsor's Plaque unveiling at Elstree Studios in 2008

Richard Todd was perhaps the longest serving and most successful of the contract stars at *Elstree* in the 1950s, culminating in his portrayal of *Guy Gibson* in the classic movie *"The Dam Busters"*.

I first met him in 1988 when I was acting as programme consultant on a two part *BBC TV* documentary entitled *"Elstree Britain's Hollywood"*.

We filmed him returning to *Elstree Studios*.

In one scene, he was walking past some sound stages where, in the background, *Harrison Ford* appeared, coming through a door dressed as *"Indiana Jones"*. I thought it would have been great to have kept the shot in, but I suspect the various permissions would have been too much hassle.

Richard was then guest of honour twice at my *Elstree Film Evenings;* first at the old Venue in the early 1990s; and, again at the *BBC Elstree Centre* a number of years later.

Richard told me he thoroughly enjoyed the many years he spent at *Elstree,* although he did recall some problems while shooting a war film called

"The Long, The Short and The Tall". The two young co-stars were *Laurence Harvey*, who was widely disliked and a young *Richard Harris*. Apparently, *Laurence* would get *him* drinking and, on occasions, this interfered with filming. *Todd* intervened one day and gave *Harris* a real dressing down and lecture on responsibility, which left him in tears, but did the trick, at least for that film.

We last met at the *Elstree Film Festival* not long before he died in 2009 when we sat next to each other for a screening of *"The Dam Busters"*. It was strange being with this elderly gent, while watching himself as a young man.

I thought *Richard* was a great chap and it was an honour to attend his Memorial Service. At the time of writing, I have recommended and it has been accepted that a road or mews on the old College site in Borehamwood be named after him.

I had the pleasure to organise a Plaque unveiling for him in 1996, when we were joined by some of his old acting colleagues, including *Honor Blackman, Bernard Cribbens, David Lodge, Helen Cherry* and *Faith Brook*.

Richard Todd and Kenneth Moore at the premiere of 'The Dam Busters'. [© PW]

Honor Blackman, Bernard Cribbens, Helen Cherry, Faith Brook, David Lodge, Martin Benson with Richard Todd at his 1996 Plaque unveiling. [© CM]

Trevor Howard

Trevor Howard was quite a character. I visited his house once in Arkley, interviewed him at his local, *The Gate pub* and he kindly attended a couple of my events. *Trevor* was quite a drinker, although his alcoholism did not seem to impede his career or acting performances.

He loved cricket and jazz and loathed *"showbiz"*, making sure everybody knew if they ever tried to do *"This Is Your Life"*, he would refuse to appear.

Trevor told me he had a great fondness for *Bob Mitchum* and *Errol Flynn*, but hated *Marlon Brando* after his unhappy experience of starring with him in *"Mutiny On The Bounty"*.

He also disliked *Frank Sinatra* with whom he starred in *"Von Ryan's Express"*, due to, what he considered, was his rude and unprofessional behaviour.

I found *Trevor* good company, but had great sympathy for his charming wife *Helen Cherry* who had to endure his drinking.

When *Trevor* died in 1988, I attended his funeral and the wake at *The Gate,* although I can't remember seeing any actors there.

Helen asked me if I would arrange a Memorial Service at the *Actor's Church* in Covent Garden. As I started making the arrangements, *Helen* called me over and said she had changed her mind because she remembered *Trevor* attending *David Niven's*, saying the place was full of phonies and never to do that for him. So it was cancelled.

Trevor Howard gave me this photo at the Gate pub in Arkley during the 1970s. [© PW]

I have attended four Memorial Services in London and enjoyed them all, if you can say such a thing.

The first was for **Dame Anna Neagle,** at **Westminster Abbey.** I was back there again a couple of years later for **Sir Laurence Olivier's,** which was the hottest ticket in town. On both occasions I went with **Elstree Studios Managing Director Andrew Mitchell.** On the **Olivier** occasion we were given choice seats facing the aisle, which proved a star-spotter's delight for me. After the service we all started to file out and I remember **Michael Caine** and **Douglas Fairbanks Jr** were behind us, and said they were popping out of a side door to avoid the media scrum. We continued down the aisle as our car was waiting out front and I remember **Joan Collins** looking splendid. Also a slightly stooped, elderly chap with grey hair walking in front of us.

During one of the hold ups he turned and smiled and I realised it was **Jack Lemmon** being very unassuming and blending into the crowd.

I attended **John Mills'** Memorial Service and on the way out his daughter **Hayley,** who I have the great pleasure to know, introduced me to her sister **Juliet** and husband **Maxwell Caulfield.**

I also attended the Service for **Peter Cushing.** I sat next to **Sir Donald Sinden,** who jokingly complained how cold the church was.

I managed to congratulate **Joanna Lumley,** sitting in front of us, on her recent OBE. **Paul Eddington** was also there, but it was sad to see how ill he looked. **Christopher Lee** gave the address

Sir Donald Sinden at Pinewood Studios in the 1990s. [© PW]

Brief Encounters

This part of my ramblings, if you are still with me, I shall call "Brief Encounters of the Third Kind" I class my encounters into three categories. The first is at events which I either hosted or attended; the second is when I have set out to interview the person; the third is just brief encounters that are worth recalling if only to add to the tally of star names in this book.

I once stood next to comedian *Lee Evans* in a studio restaurant queue, but all we did was exchange smiles.

I was invited to join *Bradley Walsh* during the interval of *"Dancing On Ice"* for drinks and he thought he knew me from somewhere, but we had never previously met. I suspect he was mixing me up with *Cary Grant* or *Ronald Colman*, if you are old enough to remember those screen idols.

I shook hands with young *Chris Fountain* at the after party on the same show and got to say hello to *Torvill and Dean*.

I once had a drink with *Bernard Lee*, famous as *"M"* in the *"Bond"* movies and once met *Bill*

Fraser in the *Red Lion* opposite *Elstree Studios,* *which* is now a *McDonald's restaurant*.

I chatted with *Chris Tarrant* while he was filming a documentary and got to say hello to the very tall *John Cleese* at the *Edgwarebury Hotel* in Barnet Lane during the filming of *"Fierce Creatures"* but remember nothing of either conversation.

I met *Alfie Bass,* who lived locally, when he came to my school to collect a visiting Twin Town exchange kid from France and also shook hands with the legendary *Mickey Rooney,* after his one-man show in St Albans.

Leslie Phillips kindly posed for a photo with me during his book signing at *Pinewood Studios.*

On another occasion there I chatted with *Donald Sinden* and told him I had recently seen a photo from the movie *"Mogambo"* signed by himself, *Grace Kelly, Clark Gable* and *Ava Gardner* fetch £700. He modestly replied *"My signature must represent at least £10 of that figure."*

Leslie Phillips OBE at Pinewood Studios. [© KM]

Peter Wyngarde, famous as *"Jason King"* on TV in the 1960s, asked me if he could visit the recently re-opened *Elstree Studios* in the 1990s. By pure coincidence, whilst we were talking to Peter, a TV in the room was showing an old 1960s episode of *"The Saint"* in which he happened to appear. What are the odds of that?.

Just after *Elstree* reopened, I spent several weekends sifting through thousands of cans of 35mm sound tracks to see what should be kept or junked. In particular, I recall locating the original music masters of *"Quadrephina"*, which the film company presumed were lost, but were about to release the film on video. They were down like a shot, but never even gave me a drink! However, at that time the studio was attracting some bookings for rehearsals and I recall *East 17* turning up. I thought they were some lads on a job creation programme.

Shirley Bassey, backed by a full orchestra on Stage 8, serenaded me when they left the doors open. Her rendition of *"Goldfinger"* was just great. On another day *Tom Jones* turned up to rehearse, but on arrival asked me if I could show him to a toilet before they started. While he was engaged, I rushed to my car where I had a 1960s photo of him at *ATV* and on his return I asked him to sign it for a friend of mine who is a big fan. He looked at the photo and joked *"Who is that good looking lad?"* and recalled fond memories of working at *ATV* in Borehamwood 30 years earlier.

I remember taking some kids, who had won a prize, to meet *David Soul* backstage at the *Festival Hall.* He was a big star following success in *"Starksy And Hutch"* with a couple of N° 1 record hits. He was a nice person, as was *Billy Connolly,* when I took my good friend *Sean Graham* to see his one man show in London. *Sean* was a big fan and I had asked if *Billy* would sign an autograph after the show. His management suggested I took *Sean* round to the stage door and the security sent a message up to the dressing room. I expected a signed photo to be sent down, but instead *Billy* appeared and said to join him upstairs where he chatted with us. What a nice man!

David Soul with competition prizewinners. [© PW]

I also met *Aldo Ray* and *Frank Gorshin*, best remembered as *"The Riddler"* in the 1960s *"Batman"* series, in a lift in my Hollywood hotel.

On the same visit, I went to the hotel to watch *The Ink Spots* in cabaret. To be precise, *Ink Spot,* as I think they were not all originals.

I was sitting on my own at a table in a fairly crowded room when the legendary tap dancer *Ann Miller* asked if I would mind sharing the table with her and her escort. He turned out to be the multi millionaire owner of a baseball team so that saved me buying the drinks.

I once met the singer *Jack Jones* briefly in the backstage corridor of the old *Venue Theatre* in Borehamwood, as I did *Patrick Moore* and *Ken Dodd.*

Dennis Waterman and Patrick Mower

A young Dennis Waterman at the Danzigers' Studio in the 1950s. [© PW]

Dennis Waterman and *Patrick Mower* played in a celebrity side in a football match I organised at *Hillside School* in the late 1970s

Dennis Waterman and Patrick Mower. [© PW]

Patrick Mower. [© PW]

Ben Shepherd, Jeff Brazier and Danny Young

Thirty years later *Ben Shepherd, Jeff Brazier and Danny Young* also played at the *Borehamwood Football Club*. What a nice bunch of lads!

Jeff Brazier and Danny Young at a charity football match.
Both would be future contestants in 'Dancing on Ice' at Elstree. [© KM]

The Celebrity Football Team gathered to raise funds for the Mayor Martin Heywood's charity.
The team included Ben Shepherd, Luther Blisset, Danny Young and Jeff Brazier. [© KM]

The Mayor's Team fielded against the Celebs.
Their manager later complained we were supposed to field older players. [© KM]

Ben Shepherd with Cllr Jean Heywood. [© KM]

Festival Queens meet the Stars

Festival Queens were chosen during a contest each year as part of the annual local Civic Festival. I used to take the reigning *Festival Queen* to *Elstree Studios* in the 1970s and 80s and I got to introduce them to such diverse characters as *Robin Askwith*, making a *"Confessions of"* film; to *Ian Ogilvy* starring in *"Return Of The Saint"*; and, to *Cannon and Ball* shooting the remake of an old *Will Hay* film retitled *"The Boys In Blue'"*

The reigning Festival Queen, Return of the Saint star Ian Ogilvy and Town Mayor Pam Roach standing in the tank now occupied by the Big Brother house at Elstree Studios in 1978. [© PW]

Festival Queen meets Cannon and Ball on the set of their film 'Boys in Blue' at Elstree Studios. [© PW]

A Festival Queen meets veteran actor Stirling Hayden at Elstree Studios. [© PW]

'General Hospital' star Tony Adams and a Festival Queen at ATV Studios. [© PW]

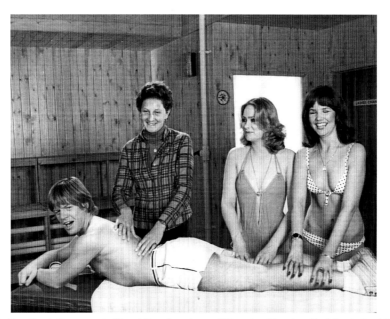

A Festival Queen visiting 'Confessions Of' set with star Robin Askwith
at Elstree Studios in 1970s. [© PW]

Festival Queen, Annette Laher, and actor Richard Johnson with stake in his heart at Elstree Studios. [© PW]

Barbara Windsor, Peter Sellers, Bryan Forbes and others mingle
with Arsenal football stars at Elstree in 1969. [© PW]

Other brief encounters included that lovely gent *Jack Warner.* I grew up watching him as *"Dixon of Dock Green".* He must have been about 80 when he finished playing the role.

Warren Mitchell naked at *Elstree Studios, Charles Dance* at the Studio and *Peter Firth* filming *"Lifeforce"* many years after making the TV series *"Double Deckers"* at *Elstree.* I interviewed him in the executive bar, as I did actors such as *Simon Ward* and *John Stride*

across the road in the *ATV* bar.

Then there was *Frankie Vaughan* at a charity event in *Elstree Village.*

I hired *Frankie Howerd* for about £1,500 to do his one-man show at the *Hillside Community Theatre* in the mid 1980s. Although his career was not going so well at the time, we found his performance very funny.

Frankie Vaughan, Trevor Howard and Frankie Howerd

Frankie Vaughan
at a function at
Hill House, Elstree Village.
[© PW]

Trevor Howard
and
Frankie Howerd.
[© PW]

Terry-Thomas

As a very young lad I had watched *Terry-Thomas* filming a scene at the top of my street for the movie *"School For Scoundrels"* in which he jumped onto a red double-decker bus.

Over 50 years later at the same bus stop, an empty red Routemaster bus, especially hired for an *"Avengers"* TV series fans' location tour, picked me up, much to the surprise of the other people waiting at the stop.

As always, the bus was supplied by the ever-helpful *Dean Sullivan* of *Sullivan Buses*.

He has also helped out with the annual visits of the *"Avengers"* and *"On the Buses"* Appreciation Societies providing old buses for locations' sightseeing.

Regarding the latter Society, it is always fun to enjoy the company of *Steve, Rob, Craig, Ray Senior* and *Ray Junior*.

Terry-Thomas, the epitome of the English cad on screen. [© PW]

Reg Varney and the "On the Buses Team"

"On the Buses" Team on location in Borehamwood. [© PW]

'On the Buses' Routemaster [© PW]

Reg Varney starred in those successful movie spinoffs shot at *Elstree* of *"On The Buses"*. He attended one of my events and seemed the same off screen as on and was a likeable person. I also recall going to *ATV* to see the recording of a TV series he was making, but there was a strike or something so they could not record. Rather than just sending the 300 strong audience home, they got out a piano and *Reg* entertained us all.

Spike Milligan seemed a bit out of it when I asked him to sign something for the archives, but he still quipped *"When they want something for the archives you know you are on the way out!"* I am told that, just before he died, he requested that his tombstone should be engraved *"I told you I was ill"*, which is great, or should I say grave, humour.

Boris Karloff

Mark Eden and the veteran horror king Boris Karloff. [© PW]

As I grew up, **Boris Karloff** was one of my screen idols, loving those late night television screenings of the old **Universal** horror films. I got to meet the King of Horror briefly when they were filming *"Curse Of The Crimson Altar"* at **Grim's Dyke** in Harrow Weald. Sadly, although **Boris** was very frail-looking and in a wheelchair, he was still the centre of attention. He died a few months later, working until nearly the end.

John Inman attended one of my **Elstree Film Evenings** and a number of years later was due to come to another, but this time as guest of honour. I sent a minicab for him, but he did not arrive although I was assured the car would pick him up any moment. A few minutes before the event and now too late to get here on time, I had a tearful phone call from **John,** but there was nothing I could do. The next day I discovered the cab driver had been detained en-route for some offence, and failed to let anyone know.

Sir Sean Connery

While *"Indiana Jones And The Last Crusade"* was filming at **Elstree**, we were collecting petition signatures to save the Studio from closure. I remember **Sean Connery** coming over and signing my sheet, saying he thought we stood little chance but wished us success. **Sean** started as an extra at the Studio in the 1950s.

Signed photo of Sean Connery. [© PW]

Richard Widmark

Richard Widmark was an unhappy bunny the only time I met him at the Studio. He was filming *"To The Devil A Daughter"*. I had always enjoyed his screen roles, so I went over to say hello. **Richard** just looked at me and said *"I should never have gotten involved in this damn picture"* and walked off. I understand he was unhappy throughout the filming and threatened to leave the film on more than one occasion.

Richard Widmark. [© PW]

Richard enjoyed a lengthy film career, starting off in the 1940s as a screen villain, but graduating into a dependable leading man and cowboy hero in such movies as *"The Alamo"* and *"How The West Was Won"*. Richard recalled one amusing incident when he was making a film with *James Stewart* and directed by *John Ford*.

"Both Jimmy and I were deaf in one ear and Ford was elderly and had very poor hearing. In one shot we were standing some distance away and Ford shouted "action" but Jimmy turned to me and said "What did he say?" but into my deaf ear so I replied "What?" Ford could not hear either of us so he screamed "Why are you just standing there you... ?", to which Jimmy shouted back "What did you say Mr Ford?" and the crew just broke up."

Sophia Loren

How did I get to meet *Sophia Loren?* Well, it was just a fluke. I bumped into the studio manager one day while walking along Shenley Road thirty-plus years ago and asked if there was anything of interest happening. He mentioned *Miss Loren* was filming on the backlot for a television movie being produced by her stepson *Carlo Ponti Jr.* I took a chance and rang his office. He said *"Sure, pop down and I will introduce you."* We wandered up to the backlot where *Sophia* was filming and had a brief chat between takes. *Sophia* recalled filming *"The Key"* at *Elstree* with *William Holden* and *"The Millionairess"* at *MGM* with *Peter Sellers.*

For the latter film, she stayed in Barnet Lane. During this visit her jewels were stolen, which made headline news. Over thirty years later, a cat burglar claimed credit in a national newspaper. At the time I was a volunteer lay visitor and appropriate adult at our local police station. One day, while I was there, an irate gent came in and confessed to the robbery as he was furious someone else was taking the credit! I don't think any charges were brought due to the period of time that had elapsed.

At the end of our meeting, *Sophia* asked if there was a local Italian restaurant and I pointed her in the direction of Signor Baffi's situated opposite in Grosvenor Road. The photographer cleverly managed to capture some lovely shots of her casually crossing Shenley Road that lunchtime.

Sophia Loren and Carlo Ponti
arrive for the premiere
of the Elstree film 'The Key'
[© PW]

Sophia Loren visiting
Signor Baffi's Restaurant
in Shenley Road
[© RB]

Anthony Steel

Anthony Steel had been a big British cinema star in the 1950s, but alcoholism and change in cinemagoing tastes had brought his career to a virtual end in the 1980s.

Years later, he was found by newspaper staff as a recluse living on handouts in London. It was arranged for him to enter a retirement home run by a film industry charity, where he died not long after.

I had met him briefly in the 1970s at *Elstree* and I decided to attend his funeral. I think there was only one actor present, a frail *Maurice Denham,* who was living in the same home and a small group of people, but no press. Forty years earlier his death would have been headline news.

Other brief encounters have included *Sid James, Shane Ritchie, Tommy Trinder, Petula Clark* and *Shaw "keep-them-peeled" Taylor,* but that is more than enough for now and apologies to the others who have simply escaped my mind.

Each and every one was a special moment for which I remain grateful and feel extremely lucky for the experiences.

1950s action star Anthony Steel in his heyday. [© PW]

Real Life Film Locations

On occasions, I drifted away from Studios in Borehamwood, prompted by some film or another. Many years ago I read that they were to make a film called *"10 Rillington Place"* with *Richard Attenborough* playing the mass murderer *John Christie.* It was to be shot in the actual street that was shortly due to be demolished, and so off I went to see the death house in which *Christie* murdered and buried various women, including his wife.

It was a cul de sac with the house at the end. I don't think I have ever walked down such a seedy road. The house itself looked menacing, if bricks and mortar can, but with a strange fascination.

Not long after, the whole street was demolished and the new layout now makes it difficult to determine the actual site.

In 1989 I invited several of the surviving *RAF* veterans, who had taken part in the real *"Dam Busters"* wartime raid, to the *Elstree Film Event.* I also invited the commanding officer of the present day *617 Squadron* and he kindly returned the compliment by inviting me to *RAF Marham.* Here I met modern day fighter pilots in the mess and got to sit in the cockpit of a Tornado fighter plane. It seemed a far cry from the old *Lancaster bombers.* The veterans were lovely old gents and sadly they are all gone now.

Rillington Place. The actual Crime Scene and Film Set for the Attenborough Movie. [© PW]

Elstree Confidential

Jack the Ripper

In the late 1970s, I heard they were to make a film at *Elstree* called *"Murder By Decree"* which would involve *"Sherlock Holmes"* tracking down Jack the *Ripper.* I took the opportunity to learn more about the Victorian serial killer by going on a *Ripper Walk* in *Whitechapel.*

At that time, especially *Mitre Square,* much was unchanged and it seemed odd walking in his footsteps down certain alleys and over cobbled surfaces. Years later I was lucky enough to be invited to tour *Scotland Yard's* famous *Black Museum,* but it contained little connected with the *Ripper* apart from a letter he allegedly wrote, which is now assumed to have been the work of a Fleet Street journalist.

Back on the sound stage at *Elstree,* I found myself walking a similar scene, but this time it was a Whitechapel Street constructed from wood and plaster, though still impressive. *Christopher Plummer* was playing *"Holmes"* and veteran *James Mason* his aide *"Dr Watson."*

James told me, *"I see Watson as an intelligent companion to the great detective, not a comic foil. He was after all supposed to be a qualified medical doctor and Holmes would not have tolerated living with an idiot."*

James also explained, *"I started my career in Borehamwood in the early 1930s but was released after a few days on my first film when the director declared I would never make an actor!"*

Jack's Letter to Scotland Yard

Whitechapel of the 1880s recreated at Elstree Studios. [© PW]

Bob Clark, Christopher Plummer and James Mason on the 'Murder by Decree' set

Dana Wynter

Very few film stars have actually lived in Borehamwood but at least one was raised in the town and that was *Dana Wynter* who enjoyed a successful career. I spoke to her on the phone and corresponded in the 1990s when she was living up some remote mountain in California.

Dana told me, *"My father was the local doctor in Borehamwood in the 1930s and as a child I remember riding my horse along the high street and in the fields as it was just a rural village in those days."*

Dana went to Hollywood in the 1950s and starred in the classic science fiction movie *"Invasion Of The Body Snatchers"* but she found the continued interest sometimes puzzling.

"I still get fans and even college students contact me, with some even doing a thesis on the film, but for me it was just a few weeks work over 40 years ago. Sometimes they will ask why did I take x number of breaths after running up a flight of steps pursued by aliens. They seem to want to hear it was some hidden symbolic message whereas it was simply how long it took to regain my breath."

Dana was a very beautiful and charming lady who is sadly no longer with us.

The lovely Dana Wynter. [© PW]

Hayley Mills

Hayley Mills

Hayley Mills is another charming and bubbly lady, who always seems so much younger than her birth certificate would reveal. I invited her to unveil a Plaque honouring her dad, *Sir John Mills,* at the studio in 1996, and when that went missing, again, to unveil a replacement in 2005. Hayley later asked if I would store some of *Sir John's* archive after his death.

Hayley enjoyed a remarkably successful film career as a child star in the early 1960s, resulting in a contract with *Walt Disney*. Her handprints are in the legendary Grauman's Chinese Theatre forecourt on Hollywood Boulevard. She also won the last of the juvenile category Oscars handed out by the Academy.

Hayley has enjoyed a marvellous career, which continues today but for some she will always be that lovely child star of *"Whistle Down The Wind"*, *"The Parent Trap'"* and *"In Search of the Castaways"*, although television audiences today know her best for the series *"Wild At Heart"*. To be talented and attractive is a rare combination, but to remain young at heart is a true rarity.

Television Appearances

Since 1982 I have appeared on television quite a few times, usually being interviewed about something connected with the studios. Sometimes you become 'flavour of the month'.

To date, I have done 4 interviews for different American and British documentaries on *Simon Cowell,* usually recounting the same anecdote of how he started at *Elstree* as a £15 a week runner and was sacked after a month.

My first TV appearance was as part of the campaign to save our local cinema, which sadly was unsuccessful. A TV crew turned up and asked me to stand in the foyer and recount the reasons why we wanted our cinema to stay. I thought I did well and this was a big moment, so I got all my friends to tune in. Little did I realise until I saw it broadcast was that I was standing in front of a film poster advertising a movie called *"Meat Balls"* and my head was obscuring the word 'meat' leaving the other word as a critical comment on my performance!

During the *"Save Our Studio"* campaign, I did interviews with American, German, Icelandic, Italian and Australian TV and even one for Brazil. In that case I was filmed mainly in long shot and they said I could say anything as I would be dubbed anyway. A friend on holiday in Spain said he saw me apparently talking Spanish on their news channel, so I managed to become multilingual without ever learning a foreign language.

Sometimes I would be interviewed in the small viewing theatre at the Studio and the director would decide to have the projector on so it would cast a beam in the background. That looked atmospheric, except the public usually expect to see the beam highlighted by smoke captured in it from the days when cinemagoers smoked in the cinema. To address this, on at least two occasions, the problem was solved by having some poor young runner lying down hidden from camera behind my seat with a lit cigarette puffing smoke up into the beam. I guess today they would have to do it with something other than cigarette smoke.

I was on a *Noel Edmonds* game show where a panel of celebrities had to guess an *Elstree* film title from the clues I presented.

In 1984 I appeared on TV AM interviewed by *Ann Diamond* and sat on the couch with *Jimmy Greaves, Doug Fairbanks Jr* and *Jimmy Edwards.*

Personally, I did not record most of these appearances, nor would I enjoy looking at them, as I neither like my voice or appearance on screen.

Radio interviews are more fun and over the years I have been interviewed by many from *Derek Jameson* and *Pete Murray* to *Jimmy Young* and *Emma Freud.*

Sir Peter Jackson

Back in the 1980s the Parish Clerk of Shenley, *Bill Ruck,* telephoned and said his young nephew from New Zealand was coming over and would love to look round a proper studio as he had just made a low budget movie.

I picked him up in my old mini and we were shown around *Elstree Studios.* He was very impressed and was a nice chap and I wished him luck but wondered if I would ever see his name up on the big screen. Well, he went on to direct the *"Lord Of The Rings"* blockbusters and gained a knighthood and a multi million pound bank balance, so well done, *Sir Peter Jackson.*

Sir Peter Jackson

Charlton Heston and Mike Newell

On another occasion, I popped down to the Studio to watch **Charlton Heston** shoot a few scenes for a forgotten movie called *"The Awakening"* and did an interview with its young director **Mike Newell**. After it was published, his mum rang me up to see if she could get some extra copies. **Mike** went on to direct *"Four Weddings and a Funeral"* and a *"Harry Potter"* film.

Charlton Heston and director Mike Newell on the set between takes. [© PW]

Characters behind the Scenes

Behind the scenes people are often as fascinating as those who appear before the camera and I have met quite a few over the years. Veteran assistant director **Ken Baker** and the great editor **Terry Rawlings** can regale you for hours with marvellous tales.

Two-time Oscar winning cameraman turned director **Freddie Francis** and three-time Oscar winning cameraman **Freddie Young** were true gents steeped in tales to tell. As was Oscar winner **Jack Cardiff** and directors **John Hough** and **Fred Zinnemann.** This list could fill the book, although, in some cases, these gents have left us without being properly recorded, which is a tragedy.

Freddie Young once told me a story about a famous actress who, in the 1940s, took a role in a film he was photographing just to get out of the country, as it was partly shot in Canada. He later asked me to delete that story as he did not like to show anyone in a bad light.

The work **Freddie** did on those **David Lean** pictures is something to behold and for many years he was resident cameraman at the **MGM** Studios in Borehamwood.

I am now involved in a project with the **University of Herts** interviewing on camera old **Elstree** veterans. **Howard Berry** and **Bob Redman** make the arrangements and the students work the cameras, sound and lighting.

This is long overdue and it is great fun listening to their stories, whether it is **Ron Punter** recalling painting *"Darth Vader's"* helmet; **Alf Newvell's** amusing comments on **Liz Taylor** and **Sophia Loren** with whom he worked at **MGM**; **Ray Merrin's** fascinating memories of being post production supremo at **Elstree**; or, **Doug Scott** recalling what **Errol Flynn**, urine and a champagne bottle have in common.

Chatting with distinguished editor **Terry Rawlings**, **Warner Brothers** publicity supremo **Julian Senior**, **MGM** prop man **Mick Brady** or the *"Saint"* production supervisor **Johnny Goodman** just reminds me of the talent needed to make a good television or feature film.

What a great bunch of men and women!

Two-time Oscar winner Freddie Francis and three-time Oscar winner Freddie Young with MGM Plaque in 1996.
[© CM]

Gene Kelly

I caught up with legendary dancer *Gene Kelly* when he was over here staying at a London hotel to publicise one of the *"That's Entertainment"* movies. *Gene* made a couple of movies at *MGM* in Borehamwood in the 1950s and he remembered being issued on arrival with a note that sweets were still on ration!

He rented a house from **Robert Donat** and was given a chance to direct a pet project film called *"Invitation to a Dance"* but it was not a success and lay on the shelf for some time.

I could not resist asking him about the famous song and dance scene from *"Singing In The Rain"* which must have been shown a million times in TV documentaries. He recalled that it was an uncomfortable shoot as he had a bad cold and the rain water was a mix of milk and water to show up better so he joked perhaps it should have been titled singing in the diluted milk mix.

Gene had a reputation as a hard task master and not perhaps a modest man but to me he was polite and chatty. The marvellous thing about those classic Hollywood musicals from the 1930s through to the 1950s was the time and money lavished upon them. Sometimes weeks spent rehearsing and filming just a two minute dance number, which would be prohibitive today.

Although *Gene* was the more athletic dancer there is no doubt the master was *Fred Astaire.* However we must not forget their on screen dance partners and as *Ginger Rogers* once said *"Remember, I did the same steps as Fred in those routines together but I did them in high heels and backwards."*

Gene Kelly. [© PW]

Ray Milland

A young Ray Milland at the beginning of his career.
[© PW]

asked if I would like to take on the part. It all happened very quickly and within a couple of years I was offered a Hollywood contract and whisked off to Los Angeles where my new life began. I did return in the 1950s to appear in a couple of movies at MGM but by then Borehamwood had grown from a small rural village into a town and was unrecognisable."

An elderly Ray Milland
at the end of his life
after nearly 60 years in films
[© PW]

I met two stars, who had started their careers at Elstree, towards the end of their lives.

Ray Milland was a leading man in Hollywood during the 1940s and 1950s winning an Oscar for *"The Lost Weekend".* He later became a successful character actor, which he told me he put down to taking his hairpiece off for the role of the father in the blockbuster *"Love Story"* in the 1970s.

Ray said his career started in Borehamwood at the end of the silent era in the late 1920s. *"I got some work as an extra and then was asked to do some effects work as a sharpshooter on a film. While working on that, the young leading man on another picture broke his leg and the director who had noticed me around the place*

Stewart Granger

Stewart Granger also began as an extra at *Elstree* but his career was really launched by *Gainsborough* in a series of popular 1940s movies. He was lured to Hollywood by *MGM* but returned to their Borehamwood Studios in the 1950s to star in *"Beau Brummel"* and *"Bhowani Junction"*.

Stewart told me *"You could say I was a difficult star because I had no respect for that old studio system. For instance I brought the idea to MGM to make Ivanhoe and they even got as far as doing costume tests for me in the title role and then suddenly decided to replace me with Robert Taylor to protect his sliding career."*

Stewart was perhaps not the most popular actor with his fellow thespians and exploited his star power. For instance he would insist on sets being built to favour his preferred profile. As his type of actor went out of fashion in the 1960s, his career hit the rocks, although he maintained his distinguished looks. Sadly, both he and *Ray Milland* succumbed to cancer and I guess their names are not much remembered today, especially with the reluctance to show black and white films on television.

Stewart Granger in his 1950s heyday. [© PW]

Stars of the "Confessions of" series after a screen custard pie fight walk along Shenley Road but the seated local resident pays no heed to such a sight. [© PW]

Filming the 'On the Buses' movie in Shenley Road. [© PW]

Sir Paul McCartney and the Elstree Youth Theatre

As a kid in 1963, I heard the **Beatles** would be visiting the **ATV Studios** in Borehamwood to guest star on the **Morecambe and Wise** show, so I rushed down to get their autographs. Twenty years later **Brian Burton** and **Allan Stronach** were running the **Elstree Youth Theatre** and they were staging the musical *"John Paul George Ringo and Bert"* at Hillside School.

At the same time **Paul McCartney** was making a film entitled *"Give My Regards To Broad Street"* at **Elstree** and the thought crossed my mind it would be great publicity to have the four teenage lads playing the **Beatles** photographed with **Paul**. It seemed a long shot, so I approached one of the film's executives and the knee jerk reaction was *"No!"* but I laboured the point as it was obvious they had not even asked him. Eventually they did and **Paul** said *"Certainly! Bring the lads down to my dressing room to meet me and Linda."* We trooped down and **Paul** could not have been nicer, chatting with the lads and agreeing to pose for a photograph which I collected after he had approved the shot.

Signed photo of Sir Paul McCartney at Elstree Studios in the late 1980s. [© PW]

Paul McCartney meets members of the Elstree Youth Theatre portraying the Beatles in 1983. [© PW]

The Beatles visit Eric Morecambe and Ernie Wise at ATV Studios. [© RB]

Paul was no stranger to *Elstree Studios.* For a number of years he had hired *Stage 5* as a rehearsal facility for his band *Wings* and also filmed the video of *"Mull of Kintyre"* there. I last saw *Paul* at the end of the 1980s when he signed our petitions to keep the Studio open.

For me it was a strange experience. I could recall as a youngster going to see *"A Hard Day's Night"* several times at the local cinema with my friends, never expecting when I grew up I would find myself chatting with one of the *Beatles.* I guess it proved the old maxim *"If you don't ask you don't get".* Incidentally I must say *Brian Burton,* who was in film distribution publicity for many years, has always been a good friend helping me at various events over the past 30 years. As the chief organiser and often host, I tended to get all the publicity but only a fool takes all the credit as most success is achieved with the help of friends and colleagues.

I must also mention *Ben Simon,* who often filmed these occasions. Utilising his creative talents he would make marvellous film compilations we could show, especially at the annual *Elstree Film Evenings.*

Jenny Ellis and *Susan Finlay* also gave loyal support and to everyone else who helped me I am glad to have this opportunity to put my sincere thanks in print.

Fans waiting for The Beatles at ATV Studios. [© RB]

The Beatles at ATV Studios. [© RB]

The Beatles at ATV Studios. [© RB]

Eric Morecambe and Ernie Wise with The Beatles at ATV Studios. [© RB]

pre-1939 Elstree Studios' veterans making a return visit in the 1980s.
[© PW]

Goldcrest Facilities Limited

Goldcrest Elstree Studios

Borehamwood Hertfordshire WD6 1JG
telephone 081- 953 1600 telex 922436 EFILMS G Fax 081- 207 0860

23rd November 1990

Mr. Paul Welsh
Entertainments Officer
Elstree & Borehamwood Town Council
Fairway Hall
Brook Close
Borehamwood
Herts WD6 5BT

Dear Paul,

Very many thanks for your letter of 20th November and your kind
remarks.

Certainly I have found the job of running Elstree much easier due
to your enormous assistance and help, not only with the Council
but all P.R. matters.

If you ever get around to writing your book, I hope you will
contact me so that I can pass on my experience of eighteen years
running Elstree and the previous period under Robert Clark.

With best wishes,

Yours,

ANDREW MITCHELL

Letter from the
late Managing Director
of Elstree Studios,
Andrew Mitchell MBE
thanking me for my help
over the years,
which was very kind.

Save Our Studios

Now we come to the *Save Our Studios Campaign.* Please notice the clever play on the initials *SOS.*

This was set up in the summer of 1988 to save *Elstree Studios.* However, a bit of background first.

In 1986 the Studio was still owned by *Thorn-EMI* with *EMI* having purchased the site in 1969. *Elstree* had been through some troubled times, never showing a profit in its entire life and by the early 1970s was on the verge of closure.

Andrew Mitchell successfully instigated a *four-wall system* whereby staff numbers were drastically reduced and by the 1980s the Studio was in profit. The new 30,000 square feet silent *"Star Wars"* Stage had been built and the pioneering work on *Dolby* sound systems proved a licence to print money.

Sadly, the corporate structure of *Thorn-EMI* was such that the film and television section seemed to sit uncomfortably and they decided to allow a management buy-out led by *Gary Dartnell.* For reasons I won't go into here, that fell through and it all ended up in the hands of the *Cannon* company.

Some film makers, especially directors making films for them, thought this was great news whilst others like *David Puttnam* could see the future. *Cannon* started with a flourish putting up another stage and bringing work to *Elstree* such as *"Superman IV"* but by 1987 their mix of overstretched finances and creative accountancy came home to roost.

First, the historic film library was sold to *Wientraub.* Then in 1988 I organised a 60th anniversary celebration at the *Gate Studios* with *Andrew Mitchell* as one of the guests. The next morning he phoned to say *Cannon* had decided to close *Elstree* and put the land on the market for £20 million.

I was shocked and said we must start a campaign, but *Andrew* said the production supervisor on *"Indiana Jones And The Last Crusade"*, *Pat Carr,* was already on the case. I met with *Pat* and we formed a small committee with the initial key players being *myself* as Chairman, *Malcolm Page* as Deputy Chair, *Pat* assisted by *Denise King* as Co-ordinator and *Sylvia Ellwood* as secretary with *Steve Hay, Paul Mitchell, Ivan Sopher* and *Peter Quilter.*

I must pay full credit to all of them especially *Pat* who got T-shirts, baseball caps, car stickers and petition sheets up and running in no time. Sadly I have not seen any of them for probably 20 years now, although I know we have lost *Malcolm* who was a true gent.

George Lucas and Steven Spielberg. [© PW]

steven spielberg

6 January 1994

Mr. Paul Welsh
SAVE OUR STUDIO
Elstree Studio
Borehamwood WD6 1JG
England

Elstree Studios is not merely a factory for film making. It has become a sanctuary of cinema history.

People the world over have been transported, touched and changed by the output of so many wonderful films from Elstree. To tear it down is to destroy a monument that your country and mine are very proud of.

There are still many movies I wish to make at Elstree. Please let it live again.

All my best,

Letter from
Steven Spielberg,
the legendary
film director

Letter from
George Lucas,
creator of Star Wars
and Indiana Jones
at Elstree Studios

March 8, 1996

Mr. Paul Welsh
Chairman, Save our Studios Campaign
Elstree and Borehamwood Town Council
Fairway Hall
Brook Close
Borehamwood
Herts., WD6 5BP
England

Dear Paul:

It certainly took some doing, but I was very pleased to hear that the Save Elstree Studios Campaign was finally successful.

I hope things continue to go well, and you have my most sincere congratulations on having rescued this historic studio just in time for its 70th birthday.

Sincerely,

George Lucas

GWL/am

P.O. Box 2009, San Rafael, California 94912-2009 Telephone (415) 662-1800

Ewan McGregor
20/4/95.

Dear Paul.

Firstly please forgive the delay in my reply. I've been on the move since January and haven't been able to keep up as best as I should.

I must decline your invitation to attend your evening on the twenty fourth of June, as I will be filming in Glasgow on a project called 'Trainspotting'.

However had I been here I would have loved to be there. I admire your work to retain Elstree Studios and if I can in any way help in the future please do let me know.

Thank you again

Much luck

Ewan McGregor very kindly offering me his support
for the Elstree S.O.S. Campaign before he became a big star

I became the *face* of the Campaign lobbying the **Hertsmere Council** and others, as well as doing countless TV and Radio interviews with crews from around the World.

I visited the set of *"Indiana Jones"* and sat with **George Lucas** and **Steven Spielberg** to discuss matters whilst **Harrison Ford** and **Sean Connery** rehearsed a scene. They had been interested in buying the Studio, but not at the inflated price now being asked. I also felt they were perhaps not that interested in owning bricks and mortar, as with most film people.

Steven kindly agreed to visit some MPs at the House of Commons, and on another occasion' the Committee also met MPs when we sat on the famous verandah overlooking the Thames.

We organised a public meeting of local residents at the old **Venue** in Borehamwiood and an amazing 700 capacity turned up. I doubt that would never happen today for any issue. 25,000 signatures were collected including **West End Theatre** casts, *"EastEnders"*, *"Coronation Street"* and *"Emmerdale"* casts.

All this activity caught the eye of **George Walker** who, three months later, offered £32 million for the Studio site.

Now **George** was someone for whom I had a secret admiration as he had grown up in the East End, served time in prison in the 1950s yet became a self-made property millionaire taking on the public school boys of the City and playing them at their own game.

He made no secret that his plans would involve selling 12 acres to **Tesco** for £19 million but promised to rebuild and modernise the **Studio** on the remaining 15 acres which was quite viable.

Many people assumed we could have protected the whole site by getting it listed, but the Government refused. In fact, their attitude was the fate of **Elstree** should be left to market forces to decide, so the offer from **George** was the best on the table.

George and Billy Walker of Brent Walker. [© PW]

Steven Spielberg pondering the fate of Elstree Studios during the S.O.S Campaign.
[© PW]

The S.O.S Campaign Committee paint out the name of Cannon from Elstree studios in 1988
[© PW]

To try to protect the **Studio**, **Hertsmere Council** agreed to the **Tesco** development, subject to **George's** company **Brent Walker** agreeing to protect the remaining 15 acres by restricting its use to film and TV production for 25 years.

In addition, they agreed to re-instate post production facilities and to re-erect the giant **"Star Wars"** Stage.

At this point the Campaign Committee, in its original form, faded away as those concerned needed to move forward with their own lives. I stayed on as Chairman and was now joined by others such as **Paul Sattin** of **Sapex Scripts** who were a tenant company on site.

We received letters of support from the great and the good and I used to write to famous names soliciting their sabre rattling on our behalf.

I recall writing to **Stanley Kubrick** asking if he could send us a letter of support. He replied asking me to draft it and send it to him. He then wrote it out in his own handwriting and sent it back to me, so in a way I had written to myself.

Stanley was a great person with loads of talent

but had personality traits that were over-indulged by the fawning film business.

I think his work, like **Hitchcock's,** tapered off in quality in his later years but there was always a new executive on the block wanting to say he had greenlighted a **Kubrick** movie.

He was single-minded with his projects and I recall his films over-running at the Studio causing problems. On one occasion the Studio almost threatened legal action due to him refusing to finish post-production work.

However, he left behind a body of work that is admired worldwide, so that is not a bad epitaph.

Elstree Confidential

By 1990 it became apparent that **Brent Walker** had been caught in a recession and were exposed to owing about 48 lenders a staggering one thousand five hundred million pounds! **George** was ousted from his own company in a midnight boardroom coup and now we were faced with **grey suits** in the City who cared about nothing other than getting back their money.

The next 6 years were a hard slog and I certainly would not have that energy today to fight such a battle. Many supporters, quite naturally, faded away especially in 1993 when the Studio was closed.

Here I must pay tribute to **Stanley Taylor** and **Pam,** his secretary, of the **Childrens' Film Foundation** who stuck it out in their part time office in the **Maxwell Building** throughout the next 3 years declining financial offers to leave. Their presence helped ensure that building was not raped as was the rest of the Studio.

Chris and Liz Clarke and **Nick Harrison** also saw it through, but it often looked like a lost cause. The giant generators were sold off, as was nearly all of the furniture, copper wiring, projection and post production equipment, carpets and even the kitchen sinks!

By 1996 the heating had been cut off and mould grew on the dressing room walls as the flat roof started to leak. The underground car park was sealed up as it was asbestos contaminated and flooded.

The studio was semi-derelict and **Brent Walker** were in clear breach of their undertakings to rebuild and modernise the facility.

In February 1996 **Hertsmere Council** were preparing for a court battle in the High Court in the Strand. One particular evening **Sir Sydney Samuelson**, the **British Film Commissioner,** and myself were attending a celebration event in Regent Street marking the 100th anniversary of the first public screening of a film in the UK.

We both got calls to say that the banks controlling **Brent Walker** had folded and offered the Studio to the Council for a knock down price.

It was a brave decision by the Council as much money was needed to refurbish the site and build extra facilities.

Painting out of the Brent Walker name at Elstree Studios toasted by Rod Brewster, editor Borehamwood Times, Gill Gowing and Richard Grove Hertsmere planning officers, Jim Hill finance director, Philip Copland Chief Executive and myself in 1996. [© PW]

In the months to come *20th Century Fox* came calling and we showed them around but they basically wanted a studio on the wrong terms.

I then got a call asking if I could arrange the visit from *Mohammed Al Feyed* and his son *Jodi*. They descended from the skies in a helicopter landing on the Studio backlot. An entrance with style I guess. I found both gentlemen nice characters, but again it was obvious they were not future partners or owners of *Elstree*. *Jodi* was shortly to die in the car crash that also took the life of *Princess Diana*. Other companies came forward, but always they wanted to sell more of the site to finance their plans for a new studio.

I was recruited to the working party to relaunch *Elstree Studios* and became Chairman of the parent company overseeing the Studio's future. Two giant new stages were commissioned, the underground car park was brought back into use and the buildings refurbished. It was truly a phoenix rising from the ashes. Then the political control of the Council altered from Labour to Tory. Although there had been all-party support all through, the new administration decided to instigate a new company structure. It was a pity, but that's life. Subsequently, to say the Council made a few dubious decisions, is an understatement but the investment has continued and today the Studio is paying back the ratepayers for their faith and is a success under the chairmanship of *Cllr Morris Bright* and Managing Director *Roger Morris*.

I ended up sidelined, but got an *MBE*. As I was not paid for those 8 years of campaigning, it was no big financial loss. I still act as the historian for *Elstree Studios* if only because, unlike many academics, I actually took part or lived through many of the events of the past few decades.

This is, of course, an abbreviated version of those eight years of campaigning and one day there is a hell of a story to be told elsewhere. I cannot stress how proud I feel to have helped save *Elstree Studios* from the bulldozers and that it did not go the way of *Welwyn, Denham, Merton Park, Nettlefold, Gate, Danzigers, MGM* and so many other studios. To all those I have not mentioned I express my sincere thanks.

To all those doubters through those troubled years, I can only say remember the maxim that a war is never lost until the last battle is fought.

A dilapidated part of Elstree Studios. [© PW]

A BBC TV crew and myself watching the demolition of part of Elstree Studios. [© PW]

I was being interviewed by a
TV crew in the ruins of
Elstree Studios
[© PW]

The two large
Sound Stages
under construction at
Elstree Studios in 1999
[© PW]

Filming at Elstree Studios
[© PW]

Elstree Studios as it looked from Shenley Road in the 1930s. [© PW]

The frontage of Elstree Studios in the 1950s. [© PW]

Elstree Confidential

A gathering I organised for one of the last screenings in the old viewing theatre at Elstree Studios in 1989 prior to its demolition. In the audience are Oscar winning Special Effects man George Gibbs, Director John Hough, Titanic survivor Eva Hart, 617 Squadron Dam Busters veterans, Lord Lieutenant Simon Bowes Lyon and a number of stars. [© PW]

The small viewing theatre at Elstree Studios. This was completely gutted by Brent Walker but new chairs were bought from a closed cinema in Paris and Ronan Willson kindly donated back the two 35mm projectors. [© PW]

The executive bar at Elstree Studios where I had a drink from time to time.
Note Dad's Army star John Laurie sitting at the bar. [© PW]

The start of building the new stages at Elstree in 1999. [© PW]

Elstree Confidential

Studios veterans and friends gathered for the naming ceremony of the Andrew Mitchell Building at Elstree Studios organised by myself in 1997. [© PW]

Showing a party of MPs around Elstree including our own MP James Clappison.
[© PW]

An aerial view of Elstree Studios in the late 1980s. [© PW]

Aerial view of Elstree Studios taken a few years ago after part of the site was taken over by Tesco. [© PW]

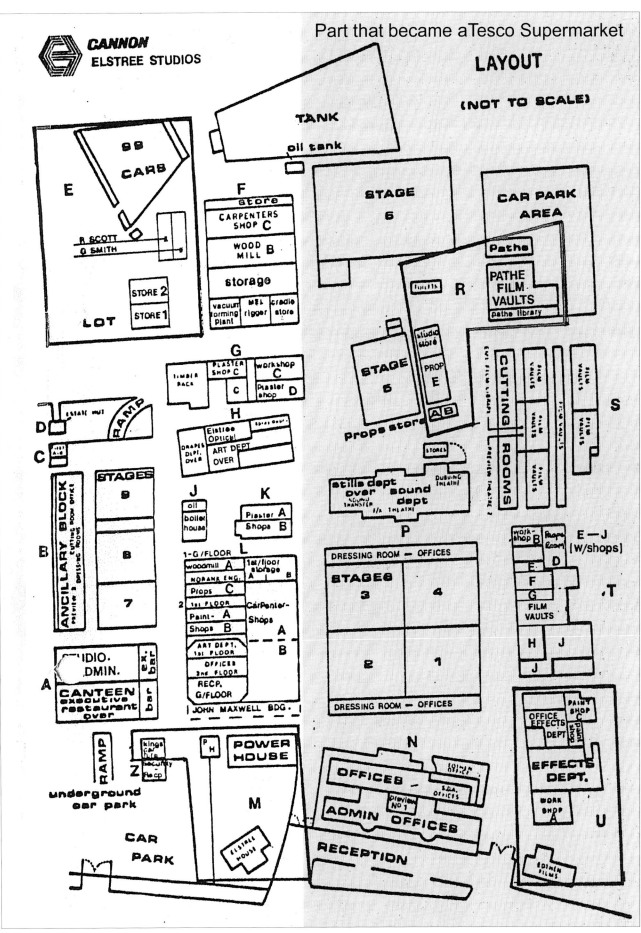

Plan of Elstree Studios showing the part that became the Tesco Supermarket

Royal Visitors

On two occasions I had the opportunity to help organise Royal visits to *Elstree Studios.* These were great fun. The first occasion was in 1985 when *HRH Princess Anne* was invited to open the new *Maxwell Building* housing workshops and production offices.

I recall attending meetings with the then *Lord Lieutenant of Hertfordshire* who was a grand old chap named *Major General Sir George Burns.* I believe he was a Colonel in Chief of a Guards Regiment and had been the aide to the last *Viceroy of India.* He reminded me of a cross between the 1940s actors *Sir C Aubrey Smith* and *Nigel Bruce*, who played *"Watson"* in the *Basil Rathbone "Sherlock Holmes"* films.

The event went smoothly and we were told that *Princess Anne* wanted to concentrate on meeting studio workers rather than dignitaries. By a stroke of luck, on one of the big sound stages, there was a large city street set still standing leftover from a commercial shoot.

In the evening *Princess Anne* unveiled a Plaque, had a tour and then met some of the staff in the restaurant.

When she had departed we adjourned to the sound stage for a party. There were at least two live bands, street market style stalls serving food from around the world and a free bar.

The latter came in useful as I was sitting at the same table as *Trevor Howard* and *Michael Winner.* Sadly alcohol does little to sharpen the memory, so most of the evening was a blur, but fun.

HRH. Princess Anne
names the new
Maxwell Building in 1985.
[© PW]

HRH. Princess Anne
Norman Harrison explains how scenery is made. [© PW]

Elstree Confidential

Major General Sir George Burns introduces HRH Princess Anne to Hertsmere Mayor Peggy Nelson, Town Mayor Eileen Stanley, and studio bosses Gary Dartnell and Andrew Mitchell in 1985. [© PW]

The catering staff on the sound stage at the party following Princess Anne's visit. [© PW]

The second occasion came about after the Studio was reopened and purchased by Hertsmere Council in 1996. I was invited to join the working party tasked with relaunching the semi-derelict studio.

My Award

I did not realise that behind the scenes my friend, *Susan Finlay*, with the aid of *Sir Sydney Samuelson,* the *British Film Commissioner,* and a number of others were lobbying for me to be given an award for the 8 years I spent chairing the campaign to save the Studio.

In 1997, this resulted in a letter from the *Prime Minister's Office* dropping through my door asking if I would be prepared to accept the award of an *MBE*. One second later, after much thought, I decided the decent thing to do was accept so I ticked the appropriate box and sent back the form. A couple of months later I was being driven through the gates of *Buckingham*

Palace accompanied by my very proud mum and good friends *Mary Albrow* and *Susan*. It was a splendid experience and I found myself strangely not nervous, which may have been the result of vodka on my cornflakes. You enter one at a time into the grand ballroom with a Guards' band playing up in the balcony and an audience of, I guess, about 300.

I was presented to *HRH Prince Charles* and he asked me about *Elstree*, mentioned he had made a private visit with his uncle *Lord Mountbatten* to the set of *"Murder On The Orient Express"* and I said I hoped he would come again. He said he would be delighted.

At the time of writing some 14 years later, I have never had the occasion to wear my medal, as I resist sporting it while shopping in Tesco, but it is a lovely honour. I realise they probably ran out of deserving lollipop ladies that year, which is why I got it, but it is something of which to be proud.

Just back from the Palace with my MBE in the Studio bar greeted by Ben Simon.
The ladies who escorted me to the Palace were Susan Finlay, Eileen Welsh, my Mum and Mary Albrow.
[© PW]

1O DOWNING STREET
LONDON SW1A 2AA

From the Principal Private Secretary

IN CONFIDENCE   7 May 1997

Dear Sir,

   The Prime Minister has asked me to inform you, in
strict confidence, that he has it in mind, on the occasion
of the forthcoming list of Birthday Honours, to submit your
name to The Queen with a recommendation that Her Majesty may
be graciously pleased to approve that you be appointed a
Member of the Order of the British Empire.

   Before doing so, the Prime Minister would be glad to be
assured that this would be agreeable to you. I should be
grateful if you would let me know by completing the enclosed
form and sending it to me by return of post.

   If you agree that your name should go forward and The
Queen accepts the Prime Minister's recommendation, the
announcement will be made in the Birthday Honours List. You
will receive no further communication before the List is
published.

                       I am, Sir
                       Your obedient Servant,

                       ALEX ALLAN

2-4 Cockspur Street
London SW1Y 5DH
Telephone: 0171-211 6301
Facsimile: 0171-211 6249

From the Secretary of State for National Heritage

97/03318

Paul Welsh Esq MBE
40 Cleveland Crescent
Borehamwood
Hertfordshire
WD6 2ER   17 June 1997

Dear Mr Welsh,

I am writing with my warmest congratulations on your award of the MBE in the
Queen's Birthday Honours list.

As Entertainments Officer for Elstree and Borehamwood Town Council, you have
been responsible for the organisation of many events which have celebrated
Elstree's distinguished past as a studio. You acted as chairman of the campaign
to keep Elstree open at a time when it seemed possible that the studio would have
to close down permanently. Now Elstree studios can once again look forward to
a future as a fully functioning film studio and you have played an important part in
making that possible.

This is a well deserved recognition of all that you have done.

                       Yours sincerely

                       THE RT HON CHRIS SMITH MP

Sean Graham, fresh off a building site, borrows my MBE at the Elstree Studio bar. [© PW]

Dressed as a Stormtrooper in the Festival Parade of 1978.
I borrowed the costume from 20th Century Fox and had to walk 4 miles in it. [© PW]

The Visit of HRH Prince Charles

My meeting with Prince Charles had sown a seed in my head, so I suggested to the then Leader of the Council, **Bryan Stanley,** we should invite **Prince Charles** to the Studios and when given the green light, I contacted the new **Lord Lieutenant Simon Bowes Lyon**.

Over the next two years, plans were formulated and it was decided the opening of the giant two new sound stages would be an excellent opportunity for his visit.

So in 1999 **Prince Charles** arrived. The management team of **Neville Reid** and **Julie Wicks** plus myself were detailed to show him around prior to arriving on one of the stages where exhibits were mounted and the guests awaited.

Prince Charles was keen to chat to the workers and had a lovely presence which made people feel at ease within seconds. We went to an animatronics workshop where he was greeted by a talking pig which had appeared in a film called "**Babe**", I think.

As you could see the workings of the pig, the film company insisted we make no mention of the word "**Babe**" so as not to spoil the illusion of reality to the kids in America who might see the news coverage. I queried "**How many other talking pigs are there?**" but it is best not to argue.

HRH Prince Charles. [© JS]

Prince Charles at Elstree. [© JS]

Prince Charles has a last word before leaving the Studio. [© JS]

As we were showing His Royal Highness around the exhibits on the sound stage, we approached a stand manned by stormtroopers and *"Darth Vader"* as a salute to the *"Star Wars"* films made at *Elstree.*

Just then a Palace official tapped me on the shoulder and said *HRH* must not be photographed with *Vader* by the press and I was to spoil the shot by standing between him and the cameras. Bearing in mind this was the *"money shot"*, as press photographers would call it, you can imagine the mumbled insults that came my way.

Further along we came across a chap dressed up as *"Judge Jedd"* or whatever it is called, a film not even shot at *Elstree.* That photo opportunity was allowed and I saw it produced everywhere from the *Singapore Gazette* to the *Los Angeles Times* but what the difference was is beyond me!

Then it was time for the speeches. Many months earlier the Palace had asked me to prepare something for *Prince Charles* which he would then modify to his own style. Just before the event *Cllr Stanley*, who was to introduce him, asked me to do the same for him and I accidentally included much the same stuff having forgotten the earlier one. On the video you can see *Prince Charles* crossing out bits of his speech as *Cllr Stanley* proceeded! Oops! but these things happen.

Afterwards, as we showed him to his car, *Prince Charles* said to me *"I understand you have been connected with this studio for a long time and I hope that continues"*, although in reality my involvement on a regular basis was already on the wind-down. I was very impressed with his sincere and charming personality and regret the bad press he sometimes gets, as I think he is a genuine person caught in a changing age.

Local residents gather in Shenley Road outside the Studio to watch the passing of King George V and Queen Mary on their way to open Shenley Hospital in 1934. [© PW]

Elstree Studios are, of course, no stranger to Royal visits. Beginning in the late 1920s the future *King George VI* made a private visit. Little did he know over 80 years later the Studio would produce a film about his stuttering problem entitled *"The Kings Speech"* which went on to garner more awards than any other movie made in Borehamwood.

His brother, the *Prince of Wales, later KIng Edward V111,* also made several private visits in the early 1930s. However one visiting royalty provoked a remark that went down in the Studio's folklore.

The *King of Greece* visited in the 1930s and was shown round by the Cockney Studio Manager, *Joe Grossman*.

At one point they stopped to look at some complicated camera equipment and when the manager saw the King looking puzzled, innocently remarked *"I guess this is all Greek to you, Sir"*

HM Queen Elizabeth, later Queen Mother and HRH Princess Margaret, with producer Ronald Neame on the set of 'The Magic Box' at Elstree Studios during a Royal visit in 1951. [© PW]

Royal party arriving outside the Studio to be met by Studio head Robert Clark. [© PW]

Tom Cruise

Tom Cruise

I guess one of the biggest stars in the firmament of today's Hollywood is **Tom Cruise.**

I literally bumped into him at **Elstree Studios** in the late 1990s. **Tom** was staying in a rented manor house nearby called **High Canons**, often used in films and TV series during the 1960s and 70s. In fact the Studio had an agreement with the owner to use it as a kind of additional backlot.

Stanley Kubrick was preparing to film *"Eyes Wide Shut"* and at one time was considering using the Studios, but eventually decided on **Pinewood** instead. **Tom** was its star and naturally attracted a great deal of media interest.

A famous talkshow host named **Barbara Walters** came over from America to interview him and I understand they originally planned to do this in the **Tower Hotel** in London with the Thames as a backdrop. For whatever reason, this was deemed unacceptable and instead the interview was to take place in a room at **Elstree Studios.**

It was Remembrance Sunday and I was attending the service held by the War Memorial opposite the Studios and then planned to creep into the room and watch the interview from the background. I noticed a big car pull into the Studio so I walked across the road. The driver had turned down an alley and had then driven off. I assumed **Tom** had been met, so I rushed into the empty bottom dressing room corridor and as I pushed through the entrance door went straight into **Tom** who was standing alone.

He said *"Hi Sir, I am Tom Cruise. I seem to be lost".* I responded by explaining where the interview was taking place on the second floor and he took the lead by bounding up the stairs two or three at a time. Seeing me lagging behind he kindly held the door open for me at the top and I took him to where the camera crew and the official greeters were mustered. They included **Jim Hill**, the Council's finance director and the man who played a pivotal role in the Council purchasing the Studio in 1996.

Jim and I watched the filming and when **Tom** was ready to leave, I walked him back to where we had met and where his car was now waiting with his publicity person and driver. During that walk, I engaged **Tom** in conversation and noticed he always maintained eye contact and gave diplomatic answers giving me the impression of a man who liked to be in control. I thought he looked quite slim. He is not as short as the press love to make out.

After taking him to his car, in answer to his request, I pointed out the Italian restaurant across the road and went back upstairs. About 10 minutes later I walked back with **Jim** and was surprised to see the car still parked but guessed he was chatting to the publicity lady.

Tom must have seen us approaching in the rear view mirror and he got out, came over and shook our hands thanking us for our help. I thought that a lovely friendly, polite gesture as we were never likely to meet again.

He was then driven off to the restaurant much, no doubt, to the surprise of the Borehamwood diners.

Tab Hunter

Tab Hunter was a pin-up boy of the cinema before *Tom* was born. A few years ago, I got an email from his partner asking if I might know the whereabouts of an obscure British film *Tab* had made decades earlier with *Zena Walker,* which he had never seen. I thought this would be a no-hoper as many such films have simply vanished, or, if the British Film Institute hold a print, it can be very expensive to have a DVD copy made.

I phoned my old friend and *Elstree* veteran *John Herron,* who ran the *Elstree Film Library* for decades. He was still then running it then, albeit from its new location at Pinewood. With a stroke of luck, not only did they have a print of the film, but they ran off a DVD for me free of charge which I sent to *Tab* in America.

He was naturally grateful and when he came over to London to publicise his autobiography, he invited me for drinks in the hotel bar. I went along with my very good pal and ace photographer *Ken Morris.*

I must say *Tab* was a delight to meet and interesting to chat to as he represented the Hollywood of the 1950s now long gone. *Tab* starred in over 50 films and even had massive chart success in the mid 1950s with the hit record *"Young Love"*. In his book he writes openly about the challenges of being gay in Tinseltown during that era and of his friendship with *"Psycho"* star *Anthony Perkins* and others.

With Tab Hunter in London. [© KM]

Top of the Pops

Back in the mid 1990s I went down to the **BBC Elstree Centre** to watch the rehearsals for *"Top of the Pops".*

I was standing on the set watching **Wet Wet Wet** singing that N° 1 hit they had that was top of the charts for weeks on end, when a young man came and stood by me.

I half noticed him, and thinking he was a crew member, innocently said *"I am waiting for Take That to come on as I have heard a lot about them"* to which he replied *"They are rubbish mate, can't sing or dance".*

I thought that sounded a bit harsh from a **BBC employee** but he wandered off. A little while later I heard the Tannoy say *"Take That to the studio for rehearsals, please'"* and five lads walked past me, including the young man I had been talking to. He winked and smiled at me and I then realised he had been sending me up. The name of that young man? – *Robbie Williams.*

As I left the studio in my old mini, I saw about 300 girls by the gate entrance hoping to catch a glimpse of their idols. I thought they are bound to think I am a TV star, so I nonchalantly drove out with the window wound down to catch the admiring screams of delight. Instead, I heard one girl say to another *"Look! Ain't that Mr Bean?"*

Crowds at the Clarendon Road entrance to the BBC Elstree Centre.
[© PW]

Crowds outside the BBC Elstree Centre awaiting 'Take That'. [© PW]

Correspondence

PETER CUSHING

21st June, 1973.

Dear Mr. Welsh,

As so often happens in my unpredictable profession, a sudden (and welcome) rush of work has come my way, which will keep me fully occupied until the early winter.

As your Questionaire will take more time than I have to spare in writing, I suggest you bring your tape-recorder to Shepperton Studios. I shall be making a film there for a month or so from about July 23rd, and if nearer the time you care to get in touch with the Publicity Department of Amicus Productions ("The Beast Must Die" Unit) Chertsey 62611 - no doubt they will arrange a mutually convenient day for you to pay a visit.

Thank you for your kind Birthday wishes.

May Success attend your every endeavour - and God's blessing be with you always.

In all Sincerity -

Peter Cushing's letter inviting me to interview him at Shepperton in 1973

Phoenix Theatre.

July 27th 1976.

Dear Mr Welsh - Thankyou for your letter - By all means come & see me - Perhaps when you are due to visit Miss Sheridan you could come & see me either before or after?

Yours sincerely,

Wilfrid Hyde White

449.5044.

Rowley Green
Arkley.

21.6.76.

Dear Paul Welsh.

I shall be very happy to answer any Questions for you, relating to your forthcoming book. I suggest you phone me at the above number and we can arrange a meeting.

Sincerely
Trevor Howard.

Wilfred Hyde White inviting me to interview him at the same theatre where I was also interviewing Dinah Sheridan

Letter from Trevor Howard agreeing to an interview

FROM 16 EATON PLACE, S.W.1
235 6879

Dear Mr Welsh,
I am sorry to be answering your
good letter after so many days but
I have been completely swamped
with work and publicity and
unable to set a date to see you
for an interview. As things
stand now I'm not sure if the
play will survive. Again my
regrets and thanks,
Sincerely Vincent Price

Letter from
Vincent Price.
We eventually met
on the set of
'The Monster Club'

JACK WARNER

7 Courtfield Mews.
Courtfield Road.
London.S.W.5. ONH.

22/7/76.

Dear Mr Welsh,

Thank you for your letter of the 8th inst.,
which I have only just received as I have been away.

There is not very much that I can tell you
about the studios at Islington except that the three "Huggett"
films were shot there when I was working with Kathleen
Harrison and other members of the Huggett family.

There were three daughters, Susan Shaw, Jane Hilton
and Petula Clark who has made such a big name for herself in
the pop singing world. The first Huggett film was called, "Here
come the Huggetts", the second was called "Vote for Huggett"
and the third was called "The Huggets abroad", when we were
all supposed to be in Africa in the Sahara desert.

All this was too expensive to be shot abroad so
the techniciens cleared one of the studios of every single
things and covered the floor with sand. The late Jimmy Handley
was in a scene with me and we were supposed to be lost in the
desert. We did this in the sand-covered studio and it was so well
done that I defy anybody to say it was not shot in the real
desert.

All I do remember is that we were all a very
happy crowd of people and the films were a big success; they
are often being shown on television these days and have been very
well received, particularly because they were just plain family
humour, of which there is not much these days in either films or
television. I don't know what has happened to the studios but I think
it is a pity they were not used again.

Best wishes
Sincerely
Jack Warner.

Interesting letter from Jack Warner. I used to correspond with a number of old stars

1O DOWNING STREET

THE PRIME MINISTER

Congratulations to Elstree and Borehamwood on seventy years of film and television production. To millions of cinema-goers throughout the world Elstree means film. We have to thank the studios there for a wealth of magical entertainment; Alfred Hitchcock's 'Blackmail' - the first British talkie, 'The Dam Busters', 'Star Wars', 'The Muppets' and so many more.

The Elstree film community has my admiration for its past achievements and my very best wishes for its future success.

Margaret Thatcher

March 1984

Letter from Prime Minister Margaret Thatcher
saluting the history of film making in Borehamwood

Star Wars, George Lucas and Harrison Ford

When I visited the set of *"Star Wars"* in 1976 I must admit I was underwhelmed by the prospects for the film. The sets looked great but when I asked the publicist who were the stars he mentioned *Debbie Reynolds'* daughter, a carpenter turned actor and a young TV actor plus a tall furry creature, a talking walking robot and a small pedal bin looking robot. True, good old *Alec Guinness* and *Peter Cushing* were in the mix but it looked doomed to a quick release and that would be it. In my defence I think many of the crew felt the same way as this was before seeing the final product with music and special effects added.

It was timely that young *George Lucas* wanted to make his pet project in the mid 1970s when *Elstree Studios* had been very close to closure and things looked bleak. *George* looked at other studios in the UK but *Elstree* was standing there with virtually 9 empty sound stages so *Star Wars* found its home in Borehamwood.

It was to make a star out of *Harrison Ford* and both *Carrie Fisher* and *Mark Hamill* have enjoyed subsequent lengthy careers albeit without the box office success of *Mr Ford.*

To *Peter* it was just another part, but for *Alec* it was something he grew to hate although his percentage of the profits made him more money than the rest of his career put together. I am told he used to destroy *"Star Wars"* fan letters unanswered and I suspect he realised that his role in that movie would overshadow all the other great work of his lengthy career. In a sense I think he may have correctly assessed the situation. When I mentioned his name to a group of 30 year olds recently they said they had never heard of him until I said he was the old man in *"Star Wars"*.

George believed in his project and its success is now cinema history. It also guaranteed *Elstree* 12 good years as he returned with two more *"Star Wars"* movies and the *"Indiana Jones"* trilogies.

I met *Harrison* again at the end of the 1970s when he was starring in the less than enthralling wartime movie entitled *"Hanover Street"* at the Studio.

Why they made that film I don't know as it seemed cliché-ridden and dated even then, but there was one good thing about it. They constructed a marvellous street set on the backlot. In one main scene it would be partly blown up in a nightime sequence recreating the London Blitz. I was asked to cover the filming by the local press and arrived in late evening on a very cold night. Setting the scene took forever and a few hours later after a lot of standing around my back started playing up. Seeing my discomfort *Harrison* kindly offered me a chair which I thought was a kind gesture and I sat back and watched a spectacular bombing sequence.

Steven Spielberg, Harrison Ford and the crew relax between takes on the Elstree Studio backlot. [© PW]

The marvellous exterior street set for 'Hanover Street' being built on the Elstree Studio backlot. [© PW]

The Blitz sequence in 'Hanover Street. [© PW]'

Years later in the early 1990s, when I was fighting to keep **Elstree Studios** from the bulldozers, I asked if we could show the three original *"Star Wars"* films on the same day at our old **Venue** theatre. They had not been released together for some years, but when I first approached **Lucas Film** they said the films were being withdrawn from circulation to be remastered and were not to be shown again in their original form. I needed a boost for the campaign so I appealed directly to **George,** himself, who very kindly gave permission and so the films were shown for the last time in their original form in the town where they had been given birth. Naturally the 700 seats went within days and it was a great day to see the fans enjoying themselves.

A few years ago **George** returned to Elstree to do a few shots on the new *"Star Wars"* films and it was fitting that one of the giant new stages was named after him.

More Films and Stars

A friend of mine, **Rob Dodkin,** has just reminded me that we and his girlfriend **Katie** attended the film premiere of the remake of *"The Italian Job".* I also remember attending the charity premiere of *"The Hulk"* with several pals including **Rick Brown** and *"Tomb Raider"* with **Matt Coleman,** but have no memory of these films. This may seem odd, but from the late 1980s I attended quite a few of these occasions and, in particular, I used to buy my ticket and support the **Royal Film Performance** each year. Often that meant sitting through and suffering some pretty boring movies but occasionally there would be a gem.

I went to **Richard Attenborough's** film *"Chaplin"* with **Robert Downey Jr** at the **Odeon Leicester Square**. In those days, the hired car collecting you was allowed back into the square and you stood in the foyer at the end of the film awaiting your turn. The crowds were still gathered outside and I remember a loudspeaker announcing *"Car for"* as they arrived. I found myself standing next to **David Attenborough** who joked *"I would be more comfortable in a jungle".* Then I heard *"Car for Joan Collins"* then *"Car for Rod Stewart"* all greeted with cheers then *"Car for Paul Welsh"* and I could hear the silent cry of *"Who?"*

"Phantom Menace" was probably the most sought-after ticket for one of those occasions and I went, dressed in black tie, with my pal **Sean.** We were dropped off in Charing Cross Road, as cars were not permitted in the Square unless you were a star. We had a drink in the pub and then had to walk the gauntlet of 5,000 fans crammed behind metal crowd barriers looking for stars. It is a very embarrassing experience when you are a nobody, so I decided the best way was to walk in behind someone famous and all eyes would be on them. It worked!.

The film I most enjoyed was *"Titanic"* as tickets were like gold dust and it was a subject matter that interested me. It was the first time I saw an audience engrossed in the chosen film at the **Empire Cinema** with prolonged, rather than polite, applause at the end. **Leonardo De Caprio** and **Kate Winslet** were present and we all found ourselves in a scrum as we exited the building after the movie.

Mike Readings and Nick Cole on the way to a James Bond movie premiere in a stretch limo. [© PW]

The most elaborate premiere was for a *"James Bond"* film, which coincided with the 40th anniversary of the successful series and was held at the *Royal Albert Hall* in order to accommodate more people. I took two of my younger friends *Mike Readings* and *Nick Cole* to give them the taste of such an event. We entered the Hall to the sound of various famous *"Bond"* themes and took our seats in the central flat area.

Mike, in particular, seemed awestruck that above us in the royal box sat *Her Majesty The Queen.* Before the screening began, *Madonna* sang the soundtrack of the latest film, then a parade of former *"Bond"* stars walked past us. I think it was the last I attended. These occasions are expensive and whilst it is in aid of charity, there is a limit. I also felt the initial buzz had gone, which had made these occasions so memorable and exciting.

Shortly before I retired from, amongst other things, running *Fairway Community Hall,* we had a booking from a television company to make a pilot for a TV series based on the *"Candid Camera"* formula. The idea was that a genuine *Spandau Ballet* tribute band would be booked to appear, but when they arrived they would find an audience of senior citizens who would show no reaction. The star of the show was *Harry Hill* disguised as a senior citizen and secretary of the Derby and Joan Club. In the audience was, also disguised, the real lead singer of the group *Tony Hadley.* It was amusing to watch the band's reaction to getting no response from the audience and with interruptions from *Harry.*

The punch line was when a planted actor in the front row got up and started dancing when he keeled over with a heart attack. I guess the formula did not appeal to the TV Company's commissioning editors as the show was not aired and no series was made

Some years ago I met *Sir Dirk Bogarde* on a couple of occasions. Once was after he gave a lecture at the *South Bank* and the other time was at *Pinewood Studios* at one of the excellent events *Morris Bright* and the *Comedy Society* used to organise.

I found *Dirk* to be a rather embittered person and perhaps someone not at ease with himself. For instance, I understood his necessary reluctance to admit to being gay when he was the *"Darling*

of the Odeons" and a pin-up to many young ladies in the 1950s. It would have killed him at the box office, but later in life and in his books perhaps not such a problem.

I did invite him to be our guest of honour at one of our *Elstree Events.* He replied by saying *"I consider myself retired from the industry and have no wish to rekindle my association with or memories of the Studio or former colleagues".*

Another gay star who had to remain in the closet during his heyday in the 1940s and 50s was *Dennis Price.* He shot to fame in *"Kind Hearts and Coronets"* but his life and career ran into problems in the mid 1950s. In fact, while filming *"For Better for Worse"* with *Dirk* at *Elstree,* he attempted suicide by gassing himself. He recovered and continued in guest star appearances until the early 1970s. I corresponded with him several times when he was living on *Sark* in order to avoid the Inland Revenue at the end of his life. Although alcoholism did not help his career, everybody in the profession considered him a gentleman and he was well liked.

During the 1970s I started to correspond with and occasionally meet some of the queens of the silver screen from an earlier era whose careers had hit the skids, but to me were iconic names. I exchanged letters with the legendary *Joan Crawford* who sadly had withdrawn from the public gaze when some unflattering photos had appeared in the press. *Joan* was every inch a film star and I think had lost her real self when she became a star as her early life had been hard. Her driver, on her last and probably worst film called *"Trog",* told me that when he used to pick her up from her rented home she would often be on her hands and knees scrubbing the floor but would then transform herself for *her public.*

I got to meet the equally legendary *Mae West* long enough for her to sign a photo. This little lady had been a sex siren many years earlier and was still coming out with one liners such as *"It's not the men in my life but the life in my men!",* which was fine when she was in her heyday but perhaps less appealing when she could have been your grandmother.

On the other hand why should not grans have a good time as well?

Signed photo of the legendary Mae West during a visit to London in the 1970s. [© PW]

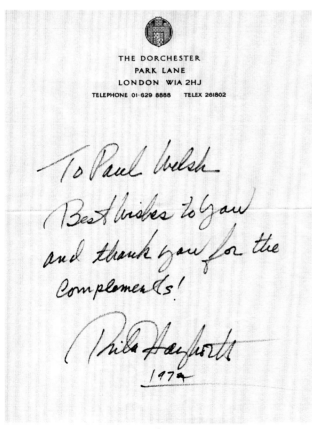

THE DORCHESTER
PARK LANE
LONDON W1A 2HJ
TELEPHONE 01-629 8888   TELEX 261802

A thank you note from Rita Hayworth
after I met her in London. [© PW]

Rita Hayworth came over to make a film in the early 1970s, but was replaced before filming. However, I got a chance for a brief meeting and afterwards she sent me a nice little note thanking me for the compliments. She only addressed the envelope to *Paul Welsh, Borehamwood, Herts,* but our marvellous post office delivered it. Sadly *Rita* was a victim of *Alzheimer's* and was reduced to less than a shadow of her former self at the end of her life.

Lana Turner came over to make a film called *"Persecution"* in the 1970s, which she later admitted was not a good film. She was a lovely lady who in the 1940s had been known as *"The Sweater Girl"*. She made the headlines when, after returning from making a film here at *MGM* in the 50s, starred in a real life court case when her daughter stabbed to death her gangster boyfriend. *Lana* also had a sad end with cancer. I found it interesting to discover that many female stars from the golden era of Hollywood were really quite small.

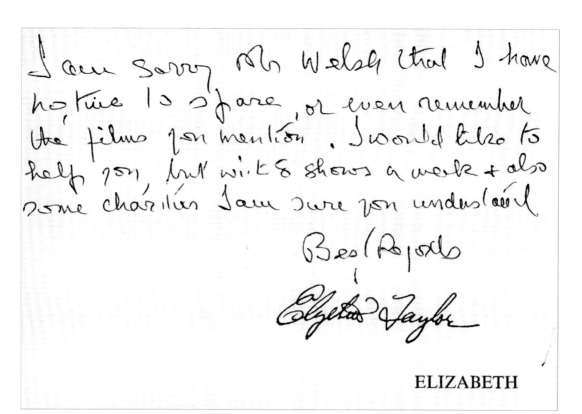

A note from Liz Taylor that did little to help my researches
of her films made at MGM in the 1950s.

JANE RUSSELL

Signed photo from Jane Russell who many years earlier had made
'Gentlemen Prefer Brunettes' at MGM. [© PW]

Signed photo from screen veteran Roddy McDowall who started at Elstree in the 1930s as a child star. [© PW]

Signed photo of Angela Lansbury who told me Elstree was the byword
for British films when she was growing up in London in the 1930s. [© PW]

Gregory Peck

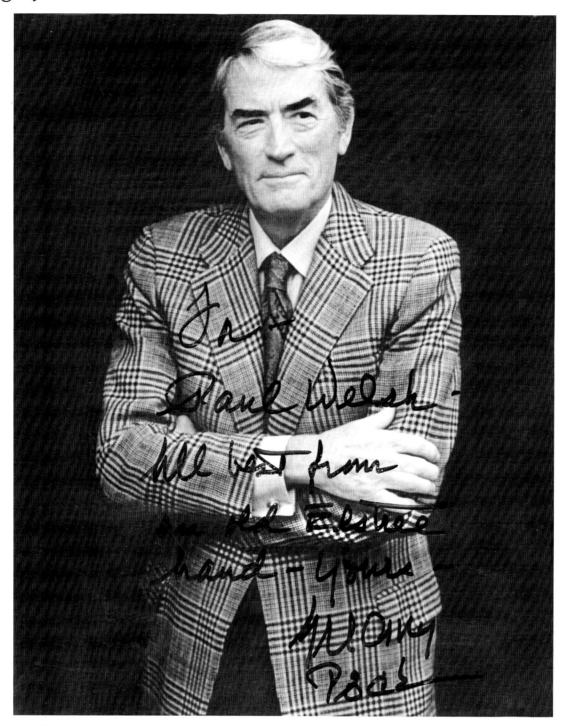

Signed photo of Gregory Peck who described himself as an 'Old Elstree Hand. [© PW]

Big Brother and the Moby Dick Tank

I guess I cannot let a book on Elstree memories pass without a mention of the *"Big Brother"* TV show, which you either loathe or love but has been based at **Elstree Studios** for many years.

The actual house sits in the old exterior water tank constructed for the **Warner Brothers'** film version of *"Moby Dick"* back in the 1950s. The tank, along with the large reservoir tank now built over on the Tesco site, featured in a number of films including *"Greystoke"* and *"Guns of Navarone"* and I remember it being used in *"Indiana Jones and the Last Crusade"*.

The tank, now home to *"Big Brother"*, was last filled with water for one sequence in the less than successful *"Avengers"* film starring **Ralph Fiennes**.

Original entrance to
Tesco's Supermarket
car park
highlighting Moby's Tank
[© PW]

Neville Reid and P.W.
filling the outdoor tank
before it became home to
Big Brother
[© PW]

The tank with the backing screen
removed at the request of Stanley
Kubrick for 'The Shining'.

Now occupied by the
'Big Brother' House
[© PW]

The outdoor tank at Elstree being prepared for a scene in 'Guns of Navarone'. [© PW]

Myself looking into the reservoir tank where the rear of Tesco's now stands. [© PW]

Some years ago I was allowed to show members of the football team, of which I was chair, around the **Big Brother House**. The thing that struck me was how small and claustrophobic it was. How anybody could spend weeks stuck in such a place is beyond me, although I guess the financial rewards, if you win, make it tempting.

Memories by Post

I used to enjoy corresponding with old film stars who were living 6,000 miles away, whom I would unlikely ever meet. I exchanged letters with *MGM* star of the 1930s and 40s *Robert Young,* later famous again on television in *"Marcus Welby MD"*. *Robert* lived to a grand age, but in some ways had a sad life which involved alcoholism and at least one suicide attempt. I remember him writing to me recalling making a film in England in the 1930s for **Alfred Hitchcock,** whom he recalled as quite a practical joker.

Robert wrote *"When we arrived Hitch invited my wife and myself to his London flat for tea. After he drank his cup of tea he went to the window and threw it out saying this was an English custom on first meeting. I was about to do the same when my wife pulled me back. In the 1980s I was invited back to Hollywood for a special gathering of old stars and the usual photo opportunity. I remember I was sitting in the front tier with Ginger Rogers and Roy Rogers was behind us and Roy's horse kept chewing on Ginger's hat!'*

Roddy McDowall told me he fondly remembered starting his career as a child actor at *Elstree* before his family moved to Hollywood where he enjoyed a lengthy career. He joked that sometimes visitors from *Wales* would say how they recognised the mining village they had grown up in, believing it was used as the location for the film *"How Green Was My Valley"* in which he starred. *Roddy* did not have the heart to tell them the whole exterior set was built in California.

Virginia Mayo recalled how she came to *Elstree* to star with *Gregory Peck* in *"Captain Horatio Hornblower"*. The head of *Warner Brothers* had seen the screen test of the proposed leading lady, *Margaret Leighton,* and insisted he wanted an actress with bigger boobs!

Elizabeth Taylor informed me she could not really recall her *MGM* films in Borehamwood, other than she was not very good in them.

Patrick Macnee wrote to me about how great the crews were on *"The Avengers"* TV series and his happy times at *Elstree Studios* and other stars kindly replied to my letters which was great fun for me

Ronald Reagan, when he was President, sent me a nice message for one of our anniversaries and *Angela Lansbury* told me that when she was growing up in 1930s London it was *Elstree* that symbolised British films.

A letter from silent screen legend Lilian Gish whose sister Dorothy starred in the first film shot by Herbert Wilcox in 1927 at Elstree Studios.
[© PW]

Lilian Gish, the great silent screen actress, recalled how her sister *Dorothy* had starred in the first film made at *Elstree Studios.*

RONALD REAGAN

June 1, 1993

Dear Friends:

It is with great pleasure that I send my warmest greetings
to all who are gathered for the second Elstree Film and
Television Festival.

This festival gives you an opportunity to look back with
appreciation and pride on the history of the studios and
to commemorate the lives of those whose vision and hard
work built them into what they are today. Since 1914,
these studios have played an important role in bringing
the entertainment of film to people around the world.
The determination and dedication which went into the
various films is reflected in the archives of the studios. I
know that your celebration also looks forward, as you
rededicate yourselves to the brighter future of new and
better films and television programs.

Again congratulations on this memorable occasion. Nancy
joins me in sending our best wishes for a wonderful
festival. God bless you.

Sincerely,

Ronald Reagan

Letter from Ronald Reagan
while he was
President of the United States,
saluting Elstree Studios.

He starred in 'The Hasty Heart'
one of the first films shot
at the Studios after the War.

His end of picture party
was held at the
Old Spider's Web Hotel
on the A41 near Watford.

Ronald Reagan and Patricia Neal
taking time off filming 'The Hasty Heart'
in 1948 to visit
the Tower of London

[© PW]

Elstree Confidential

The Rat Pack

The *Rat Pack* epitomised the glamour of 1950s Hollywood and *Las Vegas* and I thoroughly enjoyed the stage musical based on the original cabaret show put on by *Frank Sinatra, Peter Lawford, Sammy Davis Jr* and *Dean Martin.*

In fact I saw it in *Las Vegas* and years later in the *West End* with good friends *James Blackwell* and *Matt Coleman.* I never got to meet *Frank Sinatra* but did attend his last ever concert at the *Albert Hall* where the audience were still giving him a standing ovation 10 minutes after he left the stage. It is true by then he was reading the lyrics of his hit songs from teleprompters and his voice had peaked but he was a legend.

I did meet *Dean Martin* in his local Hollywood diner towards the end of his life but he seemed a shadow of his former self and I think was destroyed by the death of his son in an air crash. His screen personality was that of someone who never rehearsed and was always drinking on stage but he told me that was a cultivated image as he rehearsed everything at home and often drank coloured water on stage. I ended up with a jacket he wore in his last ever film.

I remember *Peter Lawford* and *Sammy Davis Jr* caused a bit of a local uproar when they filmed a scene for their movie *"One More Time"* at *Allum Lane Cemetery* in 1969 that involved erecting fake headstones amongst the real life lawn cemetery graves. *Sammy* was to die broke after suffering cancer and *Peter* died from a prolonged addiction to drink and drugs.

Random Recollections

As I write this book various things randomly come to mind and one is when I invited cast members of the hit *BBC* TV series *"Allo Allo"* to attend a tribute event at *Fairway Hall* which is located almost next to the *BBC Elstree Centre* where the show was taped.

The lead actors turned up and the audience came in fancy dress representing characters from the series. I had hired a local band comprising of pensioners to play for the evening. The actress *Carmen Silvera* played the wife of the Café owner, René, in the series. She always insisted on singing, albeit out of tune, and it was a running gag.

Carmen could actually sing well, but would pretend to be off key, which is a bit of an art. I invited her to sing at our event and naturally she sang off key for a laugh. However, neither of us realised the band itself was naturally out of tune!

Some of the audience with Mayor Bert Coe at the Fairway Hall 'Allo, Allo' tribute evening. [© PW]

Oliver Reed

He was an intelligent man and a fine actor, but was an alcoholic and could be a nasty drunk. I came across him twice, which was probably enough. Once, he was filming a movie called *"Venom"* at *Elstree Studios* and I was helping to show a group of pre-war film veterans around.

The second time was when I visited the location set of a film version of a *Barbara Cartland* novel. He was one of several guest stars and they decided to have a group shot taken posing with *Barbara Cartland*. They sat *Barbara* in the front dressed in pink and looking a bit regal like the *Queen Mother,* but they made the mistake of positioning *Oliver* behind her. I recall having to suppress laughter, along with the photographer, as he made various obscene hand gestures above her feathered hat.

I believe *Oliver* collapsed and died in a bar following a drinking bout while on location abroad filming *"Gladiator"* at too early an age. Some of the scenes remained unfilmed, so they magically cobbled together footage and inserted it into the scenes as if he was still alive.

Oliver Reed placed dangerously behind the regal Barbara Cartland. [© PW]

Oliver Reed playing up to visitors on the set. [© PW]

Gig Young

Another tragic actor I came across, alcohol having destroyed him, was the Oscar winning Hollywood star *Gig Young,* who came to *Elstree* to film a TV movie entitled *"Spectre"* with *Robert Culp.*

He had enjoyed a lengthy career, but obviously had his personal demons. The assistant director on the film and a neighbour of mine, *Ken Baker,* remembered him as one of the nicest actors he had ever worked with.

Sadly, not long after *Gig* returned to America he shot his new bride before turning the gun on himself.

One wonders if such people would have survived life if they had not been part of the fake world of showbiz. Or were they always destined for a sad end?

Gig Young who would have a tragic end. [© PW]

George Sanders

George Sanders arriving in England to appear in 'Village of the Damned'
[© PW]

Falling into the same tragic company was that excellent screen cad *George Sanders* who could play a superb villain, a cynical businessman as in *"All About Eve"* or a hero as in *"Village Of the Damned",* which was shot at *MGM* and on location in *Letchmore Heath.*

Arriving in England for this production, he was accompanied by his wife, *Benita Hume,* who was previously married to *Ronald Colman.*

A few years ago I attended a reunion at the village with the film's director, *Wolf Rilla,* the female star *Barbara Shelley* and several of the child actors who had played the alien children. It was recorded for *BBC Radio,* but not filmed, which was a wasted opportunity.

I also met *George* at *Elstree* when he was guest starring in the film *"Endless Night"* and he seemed tired and ill. He told me that in 1936 he had been put under contract to the old *British & Dominions Studio* in *Elstree Way,* but it burnt down so he went to Hollywood and instant screen success. I think *George* hated the idea of old age and the ravages of ill health, for not long after he took himself off to Spain and in an anonymous hotel committed suicide with an overdose, leaving a suicide note explaining he was bored with life.

James Kenney

James Kenney is a forgotten name today, but during the 1950s he played young supporting roles in a number of well known *British* films, several of which were shot at *Elstree*. They included *"Captain Horatio Hornblower"* and *"The Yangtse Incident"*. He also starred in *"Cosh Boy"* which co-starred a young *Joan Collins. James* fell in with the wrong crowd, including some friends of *Noel Coward* and was encouraged to try his luck in America. It did not work out and by the time he returned to England, his career had lost momentum.

I think his last screen appearance was probably in the *"Pathfinders"* TV series shot at *Elstree* in the 1970s. A growing addiction to drink and drugs sealed his fate and in 1987 he took himself to *Ham Common* and committed suicide. There may be a lot of glamour attached to showbiz, but there is also a lot of tragedy.

It was a pleasure to meet James' brother, Peter, last year.

James Kenney a promising young star of the 1950s who met a sad end. [© PW]

James Kenney
in the Yangtse Incident
[© PW]

Sir Cliff Richard

When we restarted unveiling Plaques to celebrate stars who had worked in Borehamwood, an obvious target on my hit list was *Sir Cliff Richard*. He had started his film career in a supporting role in a 1958 *MGM* studio based film called *"Serious Charge"* in which he sang *"Living Doll"*. At *Elstree Studios* he made that classic trilogy of early 1960s light hearted musicals *"The Young Ones"*, *"Summer Holiday"* and *"Wonderful Life"* returning in the 1970s for *"Take Me High"*.

It took nearly two years to find a suitable gap in *Cliff's* busy diary as he only spent about 3 months a year in the UK. Eventually he agreed a date in 2008 and I wondered who should unveil the Plaque. I decided to ask *Sir Tim Rice*, who readily agreed. I thought it would be nice to surprise *Cliff* by having a 1960s red double-decker bus at the Studio entrance with a *"Welcome Home Cliff"* banner on it. Then, I thought it would be even nicer if we hid a couple of his fellow *"Summer Holiday"* stars aboard the bus and *Jeremy Bulloch* and *Teddy Green* readily agreed. They were joined by *Jess Conrad,* who had appeared with *Cliff* in *"Serious Charge"* 50 years earlier. The drummer from the *Shadows* also joined us.

We had about 120 invited guests sitting around tables and after the unveiling, I interviewed *Cliff* on stage about his career. It lasted about an hour which I think was one of the longest public interviews he had done in many years. He was the perfect interviewee, full of anecdotes, but as a person he seemed slightly nervous which surprised me. *Cliff* had been discovered in his teens and has remained a star for over 50 years, becoming probably the most successful UK recording artiste ever, with hits in every decade.

Sir Cliff Richard
at his Plaque unveiling
at Elstree Studios in 2008. [© KM]

Cliff Richard showing off a car in Shenley Road in the 1960s. [© PW]

A young Cliff Richard meeting Barbara Windsor at Elstree in the early 1960s. [© PW]

Elstree Confidential

Janet Leigh

Janet Leigh filmed *'Safari'* with *Victor Mature* at MGM Borehamwood Studios and on location in Kenya. The plot involved the Kenyan Mau Mau terrorists who were in the news about that time.

The film was directed by *Terence Young* who went on to make several *'Bond'* Films with *Albert Brocolli*.

Signed photo of Janet Leigh, star of Hitchcock's thriller 'Psycho'

[© PW]

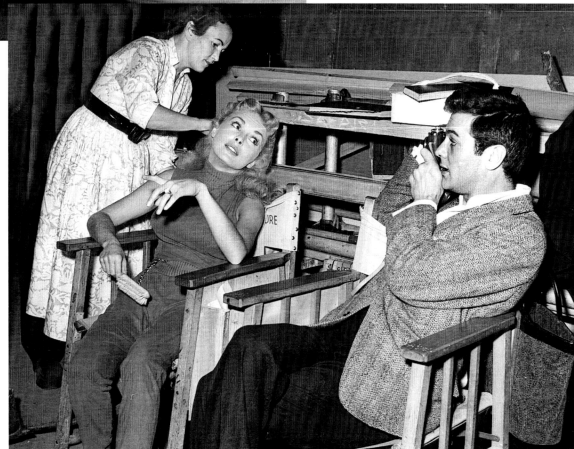

Tony Curtis visits his wife Janet Leigh at MGM Borehamwood Studios in the 1950s. [© PW]

Dame Anna Neagle, Michael Wilding and Errol Flynn

Local Star *Anna Neagle* performed with *Michael Wilding* in several post war films. *'Piccadilly Incident'* won the Picturegoer award for best film of 1947.

She played opposite *Errol Flynn* in *'Lilacs in the Spring'* in 1954 and *'King's Rhapsody'* in 1955, which was a total flop. Her husband, *Herbert Wilcox*, went bankrupt a few years later.

She was later admired for her comeback in the West End Theatre Production, *'Charlie Girl'*

Dame Anna Neagle
and screen partner
Michael Wilding.
[© PW]

Errol Flynn
relaxes at Elstree
in the 1950s.
[© PW]

Elstree Film Evenings

Back in 1984, I came up with the idea of holding a regular get together of *Elstree* veteran actors to celebrate various anniversaries of film making in our town. In 1977 I had helped with the 50th anniversary of *Elstree Studios,* but launched this new idea in 1984 with the 70th anniversary of film production, which began in Borehamwood at the *Neptune Studios*, now the *BBC Elstree Centre*.

My first guest of honour was *Dame Anna Neagle,* who had made many films here between the 1930s and 1950s. *Anna* was not in the best of health and a bit reluctant to attend at first, but her fond memories drew her back.

Her film *"Odette"*, made at the *Gate Studios,* stands up well even today and in the 1940s *"Spring In Park Lane"* and *"Maytime In Mayfair"* made at *MGM* were huge box office in the UK. *Anna* made a number of films at *Elstree Studios* in the 1930s, but we chatted about the two she made with the legendary *Errol Flynn* here in the 1950s.

She recalled, *"Errol was in need of money and a bit of a shadow of his former self when we worked together. He still had the old charm but you needed to get as much filmed as possible in the mornings as after his liquid lunches it became hard work."*

Anna was a charming lady and it proved to be her last visit to *Elstree.* She died 2 years later.

In the years that followed, up until my last event in 2008, I was blessed with the support of many actors at these occasions and it is not possible to mention everyone. However, I will mention some from my memory, at random. *Sir Nigel Hawthorne* recalled how he had turned down a role in *"Dad's Army"* in the 1960s thinking it would never last and I remember how nervous he was when I asked him to say a few words. The same applied to *Adam Faith* who remembered starting as a trainee editor in the cutting rooms in the Studios at Borehamwood, but held on to his union card, even after his first record hit, in case his success did not last.

A nearly blind *Peggy Mount* attended a couple of times and it was nice to reunite her with *"Larkins"* co star of the 1950s, *David Kossoff.*

Michael Denison and *Dulcie Gray* were charming, as were *Richard Griffiths*, *Julian Glover* and *George Baker*. *Luise Rainer* had won two best actress Oscars back in the 1930s and gave a lovely speech, still looking good in her 90s. *Constance Cummings* recalled working in Hollywood with the likes of *Harold Lloyd, George Raft and Boris Karloff* and *Bryan Forbes* recalled the time he was head of production at *Elstree.*

1989 Film Evening guests Stratford Johns, Bernard Braden, Francis Matthews, Dave Prowse, Maurice Denham, Tony Britton, Graham Stark, Janette Scott, Eric Sykes, Thora Hird, Douglas Fairbanks Jr, Dulcie Gray, Barbara Kelly, Michael Denison, Eartha Kitt, Chili Bouchier, Richard Vernon, Robert Beatty and Philip Madoc. [© PW]

Elstree Film Evening guests Sir Sydney Samuelson, Stanley Black, Ernie Wise, Town Mayor Graeme Franklin, John Inman, Ron Moody, PW, Peggy Mount, Rosemary Squires, Eva Hart, Peter Jones, Faith Brook, Sir John Mills, Helen Cherry and Lady Mills. [© CM]

James Ellis from Z Cars with Pam Cundell and Frank Williams from Dad's Army. [© CM]

Andrew Mitchell, Titanic survivor Eva Hart and Lord Lew Grade. [© PW]

Film Evening guests in the mid 1990s – spot the well known faces. [© CM]

Group shot of guests at a 1990s Elstree Film Evening – Simon Bowes Lyon, Sir Sydney Samuelson, Lord Lew Grade, Marius Goring, Hughie Green, Frank Williams, Bryan Forbes, Walter Gotell, Philip Madoc, Dave Prowse, Jimmy Perry, PW, Lady Grade, Constance Cummings, Pam Cundell, Town Mayor Leon Reefe, Nanette Newman, Jack Wild, Richard Leech and James Clappison MP. [© CM]

Group shot at Elstree Film Evening 1999 Barry Morse, Jimmy Perry, Bill Pertwee, Philip Madoc, George Sewell, Town Mayor Bill Moir, Richard Leech, Anthony Bate, Jack Watling, Frank Williams, Anthony Valentine, Nanette Newman, Liz Fraser, Bryan Forbes, Sue Valentine, Christopher Timothy, Nigel Hawthorne, PW, Andrew Lancel and Adam Faith. [© CM]

Elstree Confidential

Chili Bouchier, Doug Fairbanks Jr, Michael Denison, PW, Dulcie Gray and Malcolm Page at Elstree in 1989.
[© PW]

Gareth Hunt at an Elstree Film Evening in the 1990s

Peggy Cummins
and
Jean Anderson
[© CM]

Tony Britton, Mollie Sugden, Nicholas Parsons, William Franklyn and *Christopher Timothy* were great fun as were *Fraser Hines* and *Nicky Henson.*

Janette Scott, Nanette Newman, Nerys Hughes and *Sarah Lawson* were beautiful and *Stratford Johns, Bernard Braden, Derek Fowlds* and *Herbert Lom* were true gents. I was later invited to the Czech Embassy when *Herbert* was awarded a special honour by his homeland.

Jack Wild, forever the *"Artful Dodger"*, looked ill and *Hughie Green* seemed in need of a drink as was I! *Ernie Wise* seemed polite but cool, *Norman Rossington* and *Graham Stark* up for a laugh and *Russ Conway* turned up with his male companion. *Barry Foster* was smaller than I thought watching him on TV as *"Van Der Valk"*, but I think *William Gaunt* was taller than I had imagined.

Jean Anderson, Honor Blackman, Peggy Cummins, Ann Todd, Pam Cundell, Shirley Eaton, Valerie Leon, Dorothy Tutin, Shirley Ann Field and *Faith Brook* were lovely ladies. *Eartha Kitt* could be a handful but was charming on the occasion she attended and *Thora Hird* was just as you saw her on screen..

Bill Pertwee, Peter Jones, Leonard Whiting, James Ellis, Graham Cole, John Altman, Andrew Sachs, Wendy Craig, Moira Lister and *George Sewell* spring to mind as does *Kenneth Cope,* who starred in *"Randall and Hopkirk".*

Not forgetting *Geoffrey Hughes* from *"Keeping Up Appearances"*, *Peter Egan, Tony Caunter* and *Gareth Hunt.*

Character actors were always well represented including *David Lodge, Melvyn Hayes, Maurice Denham, Eric Sykes, Frank Williams*, the vicar in *"Dad's Army"*, *Richard Leech, Walter Gotell, Marius Goring, Martin Benson, Jack Watling, Patrick Allen, Garrick Hagon, Denis Lawson, Anthony Bate, Geoffrey Chater* and *Anthony Valentine.*

We had some regular attendees and I was always grateful for their support. They included *Barry Morse*, a fascinating man best remembered as the detective in *"The Fugitive"* 1960s TV series; *Philip Madoc* with that great voice; *Burt Kwouk,* forever *"Cato"* in the *"Pink Panther"* films, the debonair *Francis Matthews;* and, the delightful *Liz Fraser.*

They were just some of the names who came over the years and I greatly regret not being able to spend more time with each of them as so many have now passed away. From behind the camera we had Oscar winning cameramen like *Freddie Young, Jack Cardiff* and *Freddie Francis,* not to mention the great animated model maker *Ray Harryhausen* and the co-creator of *"Dad's Army"*, *Jimmy Perry*. We even had *Lord Lew Grade* attend a couple of times. He was forever linked with *ATV* in Borehamwood and on receiving the peerage took the title *Baron of Elstree.*

I found hosting these occasions great fun and although many of these guests are now half forgotten, it was a pleasure for me to meet them. They happened at just the right time as today's stars have not got the same nostalgic view of the old studios of Borehamwood, so such events can never really happen again.

Peter Waterman OBE
[© CM]

Wendy Craig and Herbert Lom at an
Elstree Film Evening
[© CM]

Honor Blackman,
Barry Morse and
Constance Cummings
at a 1990s
Elstree Film Evening
[© CM]

Mollie Sugden
[© CM]

Commemorative Plaques

In 1996 the **British Film Institute** decided to celebrate the Centenary of cinema in various ways, including offering free commemorative Plaques for anyone who could nominate a film related site around the UK.

There were to be 200, so I applied for Borehamwood and we ended up with 10 per cent of them! The only catch was I would have to organise a suitable unveiling ceremony for each of the 20 Plaques.

Luckily **Elstree & Borehamwood Town Council** agreed to allow me the time to do so and **Neville**

Reid, the Managing Director at **Elstree Studios,** permitted several to be staged at the Studios.

The one at **Elstree** for **Sir John Mills** was good fun as he was such a gentleman and it was great that **Hayley Mills** joined him to unveil the Plaque.

John recalled that over 60 years earlier he had worked at the Studio with the comedy actor **Will Hay** and had learnt more about timing and screen acting technique than he would have done in two years at RADA.

Sir John Mills and Hayley Mills

PW with Lady and Sir John Mills and Hayley Mills
at his Plaque unveiling at Elstree Studios in 1996
[© CM]

Sir John also remembered filming the final scene in *"Ice Cold In Alex"* where they arrive in a bar and he downs an ice cold glass of lager in one. They had tried various fake drinks but in the end decided to use the real thing. The problem was it required several takes and as John recalled *"I was absolutely plastered and had to be taken to my dressing room to lay down. The only time I have been drunk on a film set."*

As I walked him to his car after the ceremony, he said *"Don't forget if they have any roles for an old actor remember me."* It was to be his last visit to *Elstree,* although he continued acting almost up until his death, despite severe sight problems.

That year *Honor Blackman* unveiled a Plaque honouring *Elizabeth Taylor* and *Sylvia Syms* did the one for *Elstree Studios* taking the opportunity to remark *"We carry on about stars but the most important thing is the film crews and the ones here were the best."*

Christopher Lee unveiled the one for his old co-star and friend *Peter Cushing* and spoke eloquently for 20 minutes, much to my surprise, as I was holding up the heavy metal Plaque.

Bill Owen MBE

In 1996 we also put Plaques at the locations of the *Danziger Studios* with *Sir Sydney Samuelson,* the *MGM* site with two time Oscar winner *Freddie Francis* and three time Oscar winner *Freddie Young* and one for the first Studio, *Neptune,* at the *BBC Elstree Centre.*

For the latter my idea was to have two unveilers representing past and present. I asked *Bill Owen,* best remembered for *"Last of the Summer Wine",* who had starred in films at the Studio in the 1940s and teenage heartthrob of *"EastEnders",* *Paul Nicholls.*

Being an old professional, *Bill* turned up on the appointed day, but no sign of *Paul* despite Tannoy calls around the site. I later found out he had gone home and forgotten about the event. The following day he was very apologetic and we did some photos of him also unveiling the Plaque. Incidentally, not long after, they filmed the interiors of some episodes of *"Last of the Summer Wine"* at *Elstree Studios* and *Bill* invited me to visit the set. It was an odd experience sitting in that famous café and seeing those familiar characters.

Bill Owen at BBC Elstree Centre in 1996. [© CM]

Paul Nicholls at the BBC Elstree Centre in 1996.[© CM]

The BBC Elstree Centre when it was the Rock Studios in the 1930s
and Neptune Studios before that. [© PW]

We also did a Plaque at *Imperial Place Office* complex celebrating the old *British & Dominions Studio* that had stood on the site until badly damaged by fire in 1936. It was at this Studio that *Douglas Fairbanks,* the great silent screen Hollywood star, made his last ever film and where *Korda* produced the Oscar winning *"The Private Life of Henry VIII"*. It was unveiled jointly by silent screen star *Chili Bouchier, Tommy Ibbetson*, who had been a page boy at the Studio and *Elizabeth and John Wilcox.*

Tommy Ibbetson, Elizabeth Wilcox, Chili Bouchier and John Wilcox at B and D Studio Plaque unveiling. [© CM]

Chili Bouchier in her 1930s heyday. [© PW]

Ralph Fiennes

PW and Ralph Fiennes at the 1997 Charles Laughton Plaque unveiling at Elstree Studios. [© CM]

Most of the Plaques were unveiled in a flurry of activity in 1996, as I juggled dates and guest unveilers.

In 1997 *"Schindler's List"* star *Ralph Fiennes* accepted my invitation to unveil one for *Charles Laughton.* Then I was lucky enough to get *Olivia De Havilland* to do the one for her old *"Gone With The Wind"* co-star *Vivien Leigh* who had started at *Elstree. Olivia* came over from Paris and was staying with relatives over Aylesbury way so I went by car to collect her. What a charming lady and still glamourous in her eighties. I asked if she had kept in touch with her co-stars after films were made, such as *Errol Flynn* and *Clark Gable.*

To my surprise she replied *"I had a meal with Clark in 1940 a year after we had finished "GWTW" but our paths never crossed again before his death 20 years later. I made several films with Errol in the 1930s and had a big crush on him, but he was the kind of man you should never marry. He was charming and handsome with a wicked sense of humour. In the 1950s I had moved to Paris, but was invited back to attend a social event in Hollywood. During the evening I felt a tap on the shoulder and someone said "Hello Sport". I turned round and for a couple of seconds did not recognise the man, then realised it was Errol. The once sparkling eyes seemed dead and his face bloated. It was very sad."*

Olivia had been under long term contract to *Warner Brothers* and fought the Studio about such contracts, thereby falling out with the boss *Jack Warner.*

When I introduced *Olivia*, I quoted *Mr Warner* saying *"If you think Bette Davis is a tough broad you have never met De Havilland",* to which *Olivia* roared with laughter. A lovely lady from Hollywood's golden era.

PW and Olivia de Havilland at the Vivien Leigh Plaque unveiling at Elstree Studios in 1998. [© PW]

Stanley Kubrick

One of the final Plaques in the original group of unveilings came about in 1999, as I still had one for **Stanley Kubrick**, but the director was not keen on such publicity. After he had completed *"Eyes Wide Shut"*, I did ask **Tom Cruise** but got a message back declining. Then by chance I heard that *"Clockwork Orange"* star **Malcolm McDowell** was filming a guest star role in a movie at **Elstree,** but this was his last day. I had been gardening on a day off, so rushed to the office, picked up the Plaque and rushed to the **Studio** where **Malcolm** kindly 'unveiled' the Plaque, albeit in a ceremony consisting of just the two of us and a photographer.

PW with Malcolm McDowell on the set of 'Gangster No.1' at Elstree Studios with the Kubrick Plaque.
[© PW]

Lord Richard Attenborough and Bryan Forbes CBE

The final Plaque unveilings I hosted were in 2008 when we did four in one year. I have mentioned *Cliff Richard,* but I also enjoyed inviting back *Bryan Forbes* to be a recipient with his charming wife *Nanette Newman.* Then, I wondered who could I ask to be the guest unveiler and a natural choice was his old friend *Lord Richard Attenborough,* who readily agreed.

We decided to make his appearance a secret, which involved hiding *Richard* at the *Studio* and making sure they did not arrive at the same time.

After the unveiling I interviewed both gentlemen on stage and I felt quite privileged having seen them both in so many films including one of my favourites *"League Of Gentlemen"*

Interviewing Bryan Forbes and Lord Richard Attenborough at Elstree Studios in 2008. [© PW]

Bryan Forbes CBE and BBC Radio staff at Elstree Studios' Reopening. [© PB]

Barbara Windsor MBE

The Plaque for *Barbara Windsor* was a good laugh and it was nice to meet her husband *Scott* for the first time. On this occasion I invited the director of her *Elstree* made film *"Crooks in Cloisters"*, *Jeremy Summers*, to be the unveiler and invited some of her showbiz colleagues including *Dale Winton, Pam St Clement* and the wonderful *Stanley Baxter*. *Barbara* is a true delight to work with as she is such a 'people person'. After the interview, she insisted that she wanted to go round the tables to meet all the community guests.

Signed 'thank you' photo from Barbara Windsor after organising her Plaque unveiling in 2008.
[© PW]

Sir Christopher Lee

My final Plaque of the series was one that had lain in the cupboard for several years as the recipient was so hard to pin down. It was *Christopher Lee* and the unveiling was a last minute affair.

The annual *Elstree Film Evening* was taking place and a few days before *Christopher* phoned me to say he could attend. I hastily rearranged the second half to accommodate the unveiling on stage and invited his old *Hammer* co-stars *Francis Matthews* and *Barbara Shelley* to be the unveilers.

They are both great ambassadors for the acting profession and I know *Christopher* was very moved by the kind remarks *Barbara* made about working with him.

I think it was a good one to end on and I hope I did them all justice.

Liz Fraser, Sylvia Syms OBE,
Sir Christopher Lee
standing with knees bent
and myself
at the re-opening
of Elstree Studios
in 1996. [© CM]

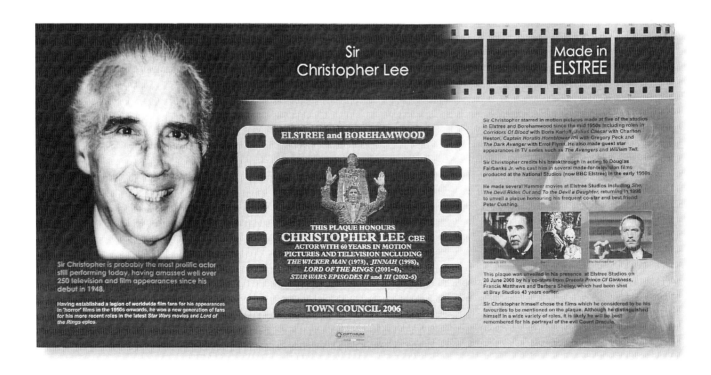

Further Commemorative Plaques

Simon Cowell

In 2006 I recommended that we recommenced the programme of Commemorative Plaque unveilings that had first been undertaken between 1996 and 1998. These took place at *Elstree Studios* and I thoroughly enjoyed the challenge of organising and hosting the occasions. My desire was to start with two high profile recipients mixing the past with the present.

It crossed my mind that we needed to interest younger people in these proceedings, so my first target was the music mogul *Simon Cowell*. All the Plaques honoured people who had worked in the studios of Borehamwood. *Simon* had started his showbiz career at *Elstree Studios* in the late 1970s as a runner on *"The Return Of The Saint"* TV series. He earned £15 a week, but was sacked after a month and decided to ask his dad to get him into the music industry instead. He is now the most famous and most powerful producer and TV star in the world. *Simon* grew up in Barnet Lane, Elstree. His parents later sold their house to legendary film director *Stanley Kubrick.*

I must admit I did not particularly warm to his television image before we met but *"X Factor"* had made him a hit especially with my younger friends so I wrote asking if he would agree to be a Plaque recipient and attend a ceremony. To ensure he actually got the letter, my friend *John West*, who was part of the management team that ran the TV studio where *"X Factor"* was made, agreed to hand it to him personally.

A few days later *Simon* wrote saying he was flattered and would be honoured, so I approached his old mentor *Peter Waterman* to be the surprise guest unveiler and he agreed. On the day itself *Simon* was fashionably late, but he charmed everyone and proved to be a really nice guy. A local singer, *Rob Dodkin,* bravely performed a song he had especially written and our local Community Choir sang a version of *"My Way"* with the lyrics comically rewritten and the song retitled *"Si's Way".*

A few days later, I received a letter from *Simon* saying how moved he had been by the occasion and by the effort everyone had put in. He commented this was the first *"Award"* he had received and it brought back memories of how he had started in showbiz. Perhaps we had a glimpse of the real man behind the panto villain we see on our screens.

PW with music mogul Simon Cowell at his Elstree Studios Plaque unveiling in 2006. [© KM]

Simon Cowell kindly inscribed a copy of his book for me after his Plaque unveiling

Sir Roger Moore

The second recipient was also no stranger to **Elstree Studios,** having spent most of the 1960s starring in the hit TV series *"The Saint"* and of course it was **Sir Roger Moore.**

I approached him via another friend, **Gareth Owen,** who had become his assistant in the UK and I first met when he was a young student helping us collect petition signatures to save the Studios nearly 20 years earlier.

Roger also made the pilot episode of the *"Ivanhoe"* TV series at **Elstree** in the 1950s and many years later made a couple of good films at the Studios including *'The Man Who Haunted Himself'.*

My idea on this occasion was to make it a *"Saint Reunion",* so I invited various guest stars from the series along with key crew members to join us.

We also invited the Series' 90 year old producer **Bob Baker** to be the guest unveiler. It was a lovely surprise for **Roger,** who is universally liked in the profession, not least for the fun he used to bring to the set when filming.

I even managed to get a couple of white 1960s Volvo sports cars to be parked at the Studio entrance. This was the iconic vehicle *"The Saint"* drove in the series after British car companies declined to provide a vehicle for the filming, on the grounds they were already selling enough of their cars. Those were the days!

SIR ROGER MOORE PLAQUE UNVEILING - 31st OCTOBER 2006

Top row from left to right - JOHN GROVER, JIMMY DEVIS, ALAN HUME, JOHN HOUGH, PETER MANLEY, MARCIA STANTON, RAY LONNEN, JAN WILLIAMS, EUNICE GAYSON, JEREMY SUMMERS, PHILIP MADOC, MADELINE KELLOCK, JUNE RANDALL, MALCOLM CHRISTOPHER, KEN BAKER & MIKE REED
Bottom row - TONY ARNELL, DAVE PROWSE, LADY KRISTINA MOORE, SIR ROGER MOORE, BOB BAKER, JOHNNY GOODMAN, FRANCIS MATTHEWS & BURT KWOUK

Sir Roger Moore and other Saint veterans at the reunion I organised in 2006
[© KM]

Signed "Thank you" photo from
Sir Roger Moore
after his
Plaque unveiling
in 2006.
[© PW]

Sir Roger Moore
at his Plaque unveiling
in 2006.
[© KM]

Once more I used the **Borehamwood Community Choir** to perform a musical tribute; this time using a re-worded medley of **"James Bond"** songs.

Roger was very moved by this and he sent me a lovely letter afterwards saying what a great occasion it had been.

These occasions were put on, in budget terms, for peanuts, but with a great deal of goodwill and in the knowledge they could never be repeated.

Escorting Sir Roger and Lady Moore into Elstree Studios on his first visit for over 30 years, in 2006. [© KM]

Flashback to earlier days. Visitors meeting Charlie Drake, Roger Moore and Steve Forrest
by the Elstree Studios' Managers' house. Roger is talking to Toni Gardener who became Queen of Jordan
[© PW]

Elstree Confidential

The same visitor with Steve 'The Baron' Forrest and Yul Brynner. [© PW]

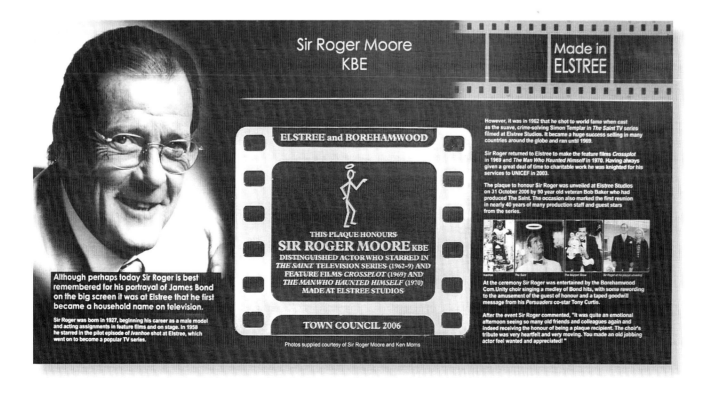

Sir Michael Caine

My meeting with *Michael Caine*, in his pre knighthood days, was a pure photo opportunity I conjured up.

I was publicising a Studio anniversary and I visited him on the set of *"The Fourth Protocol"* in the 1980s. I took with me an aerial shot of the Studio in the 1930s and a photographer took some snaps of us looking at it.

Michael had begun as an extra at the Studio in the 1950s but has hardly made any films here since.

He was taller than I imagined and put up with me. I seem to remember he mentioned wearing mascara when being filmed, as it highlighted his eyelashes, which would otherwise not photograph well.

Of course, he was also famous as being the first leading man to wear glasses on screen, probably since the days of *Harold Lloyd,* and has enjoyed a lengthy career neatly shifting from leading man to star character actor.

PW and Sir Michael Caine on the set of 'The Fourth Protocol' at Elstree Studios. [© PW]

Some Interviews

I did a number of interviews with actors, both at *Elstree* and across the road at *ATV,* and some spring to mind as I write.

Edward Woodward was a nice chap and not at all like the TV character of *"Callan"* he portrayed so well. I recall us talking about his rock collection and other hobbies.

Hollywood tough guy *Sterling Hayden* held strong views on various people he had worked with in past years. He described *Joan Crawford* as a bitch and said he would never work with *Stanley Kubrick* again.

Sterling played the mad airforce officer in *"Dr Strangelove"* who unleashed the atom bombs on Russia.

He recalled *"Kubrick had me do a scene in which I break down about 50 times and I was at my wits end as to what he wanted from me. After the final take he said "That's fine" and I asked him what was the damn difference between that and take one or ten. Kubrick said "I wanted to capture the real panic and frustration in your eyes!", "Would the public care whether I acted it or felt it?",* Sterling doubted.

I have only come across a couple of *snappy* stars in all these years thank goodness. One that springs to mind was *Leo McKern.* When I used his Christian name on the occasion of us meeting for the first time, he considered I was being disrespectful, whereas I thought I was being friendly!.

On another occasion I wrote to an actress who was a *Dame* and dared to use her first name. Her secretary phoned to say this particular lady felt it proper she was always addressed as *Dame...* but I won't mention her name. Titles sometimes go to people's head.

I always thought *Lew Grade* was the last of the true television moguls and certainly the last of its characters. He was in at the beginning of Independent Television and his *ATV Studios* in Borehamwood produced thousands of programmes in its 23-year history. The screenwriter and mastermind behind the *"Avengers"* told me a story, which summed *Lew* up.

Brian Clemens recalled *"Lew called me in to his office and asked if I would write a new thriller series for TV. I said yes, but where was the contract? and What would I be paid? Lew replied "Don't worry my boy you will be happy" and on that basis I went off and wrote several episodes before ever seeing a contract. He was right, I was happy, but that kind of management would never be allowed today."*

Lew was a guest at a couple of occasions I organised, along with his trademark cigar. He remained active until the end and I attended his Memorial Service held at a London theatre. On the way out I passed a fellow attendee actor, *Ian Bannen,* who I had always wanted to meet, but we just smiled and said "Hello". Later Ian was tragically killed in a road accident.

Other names cross my mind, as I consume a bottle of red wine. Alcohol must be good for kick-starting the memory cells.

I remember *Leonard Rossiter* on location at *Brookside Boys Club,* when he was making the film version of *"Rising Damp"* based on a TV series I much enjoyed. I found *Leonard* to be a rather serious character off screen, as many comedians seem to be.

I went down to *Elstree Studios* and visited the sets of the film versions of *"Are You Being Served"* about which I recall little and *"George And Mildred"* where I met *Brian Murphy* and *Yootha Joyce,* who were happy to be interviewed. Sadly, I think *Yootha* had a drink problem and died long before her time.

Arthur Askey

I came across *Arthur Askey* at *ATV* waiting to appear on *"Celebrity Squares"* and again not long after at *Elstree* on the film *"Rosie Dixon, Night Nurse"*. The title sums up the movie. *Arthur* was very bubbly and friendly and recalled when he first starred in films:

"I was a big star on radio but except for press photos the public had not really seen me and did not realise how short I was.

Then I got offered a starring role in a film. When it was released, I sneaked into a cinema and happened to sit behind two ladies hoping to hear flattering comments about my performance. Instead, as the film ended, one turned to the other and said "I never realised he was deformed", referring to my height!

Arthur Askey and the girls from 'Rosie Dixon, Night Nurse', another Elstree Classic. [© PW]

Old-time entertainer
Arthur Askey had kept the country cheerful during war-time with his West End Theatre performances.

Shown here with long-time Boreham Wood resident and actress Eileen Tatler, appearing in 'Follow the Girls'

[© SAL]

Margaret Lockwood

Another star of yesteryear I met whilst waiting to appear on the same *ATV* production, was *Margaret Lockwood* who became famous in the 1940s.

She told me *"I actually almost began my career at Elstree in the 1930s when I auditioned for a role. The casting director insisted I shaved off my eyebrows. I did not get the part and the eyebrows never grew back".*

It will be difficult for younger readers to appreciate that Margaret was a big star in her heyday of the 1940s, ranking Nº 1 female star at the UK box office at one time. Her stardom began in the 1930s with Hitchcock's *"The Lady Vanishes"* and cemented with starring roles in several *Gainsborough Studio* films such as *"The Wicked Lady"* and *"The Man In Grey".* They can look dated now but were huge successes in their day.

Her screen career had all but petered out by the 1960s, although she continued on stage and television. Sadly, in her latter years, she suffered from hearing problems and was a virtual recluse for nearly a decade before her death in 1990.

Anna Neagle, Margaret Lockwood and Herbert Wilcox at Elstree in the early 1950s. [© PW]

Bob Monkhouse

Bob Monkhouse was the host of *"Celebrity Squares"*, as he was of other *ATV* productions, such as *"The Golden Shot"* and *"Family Fortunes"*.

You either loved or hated him as he tended to come across as smug, which is not the best image. He was actually a nice chap and highly intelligent with a great talent for comedy. I saw a number of those shows recorded and *Bob* could also be a bit blue in his humour during warm up sessions, but had a razor sharp mind.

I also remember going to *ATV* to see a couple of episodes of *"Family Fortunes"* after *Max Bygraves* had taken over as host. One episode had everybody in hysterics, including *Max,* when the contestant, presumably out of a mental block induced by fear, answered "chicken" to every question. On another occasion a contestant was asked to name something made out of rubber and answered "condom" which in those innocent days was a no-no during family viewing and I believe the episode was scrapped.

BOB MONKHOUSE

Paul Welsh Esq.,

BOREHAMWOOD. HERTS.   3rd December, 1985.

Dear Paul,

Thank you for your letter with regard to the Gala evening you intend to hold during February and April.

As much as I would like to help I am afraid my commitments prevent it.   I am currently in the middle of recording my BBC2-TV series which takes a Christmas break this week when I shall then fly off to take in some winter sunshine. On my return we complete the series during Jan/ Feb and March and then I have to go to Los Angeles to do some taping there....Returning in mid-April to start recording 'Bob's Full House' plus fulfilling a number of already contracted cabaret dates. *PHEW !*

Please forgive my failure to help on this occasion.

Yours sincerely,

Bob Monkhouse

Letter from Bob Monkhouse

Dinah Sheridan

Signed photo of
Dinah Sheridan
star of 'Genevieve'.
[© PW]

Dinah Sheridan, was considered to be the quintessential English Rose. She had Russian and German parents. I interviewed her in her theatre dressing room and we chatted about her most famous film, the comedy *'Genevieve".*

She said *"That was a low budget effort and when the Rank Organisation saw the finished film they hated it and wanted to have it scrapped. Eventually they released it and it became a 1950s classic."*

Sir Alfred Hitchcock

Alfred Hitchcock
at Elstree Studios in 1949
[© PW]

Blackmail star, Anny Ondra, who later married
Max Schmeling, German World Heavyweight Boxing champion.
[© PW]

Alfred Hitchcock I met briefly on the set of *"Frenzy"* in London and by that time I think he was probably long past his best, both health and career wise. I got the impression he had shot the film already in his head and the actual filming held little real interest for him.

Hitch, of course, had made a name for himself at *Elstree Studios* in the late 1920s and early 30s as the wonder boy director and directed the first *British sound film* here called *"Blackmail"*. During production of what started as a silent film, the craze for talkies arrived, so *Hitch* added sound sequences on a hastily constructed sound stage. *Hitch* used to love practical and sometimes cruel jokes.

One veteran told me, *"He was directing a film which involved a graveyard scene and he bet a burly East End stagehand that he would be too frightened to stay on the set overnight. The man said he would take the bet but, Hitch insisted he be handcuffed to the set in case he crept off during the night. The stagehand readily agreed and then Hitch left him a flask of tea to keep him warm. What the stagehand did not know was the tea was laced with a strong laxative and you can imagine the scene the next morning!"*

On *"Blackmail"*, Hitchcock had a problem, insofar as the leading lady *Anny Ondra* had a thick Eastern European accent, totally wrong for her character. This was before the art of dubbing. The solution was to have another English actress in front of a mike, just off camera, saying the lines as *Anny* mimed them.

Hitchcock returned to *Elstree Studios* to make *"Stage Fright"* with *Marlene Dietrich* after the War and to *MGM* in *Elstree* to film *"Under Capricorn"* with *Ingrid Bergman.* Her co-star in the film *Joseph Cotton* told me it was not a successful film and he called it *"Under corny crap".*

Ingrid Bergman

I did get to meet *Ingrid Bergman* on the set of *"Murder On The Orient Express"* at *Elstree.* She was a charming lady and I could not resist asking her about the famous movie *"Casablanca"* in which she starred with *Bogart.*

She recalled it was not a fun picture to make, as *Bogart* was often distracted by rows with his then wife. The script was still being altered as they filmed, so she did not know when playing her character if she was supposed to end up with *Bogart* or *Paul Henreid*.

Ingrid also recalled the Studio boss hated the now famous song *"As Time Goes By"*.

The actor cast as the piano player in *"Rick's Café"* to whom she uttered the immortal lines *"Play it, Sam"* could not play a piano, so it had a wooden keyboard and he pretended.

Cary Grant and Ingrid Bergman meet a London Bobby on location. while filming 'Indiscreet, in 1957.
[© PW]

Valerie Hobson

Another nice lady I met was actress *Valerie Hobson* who started her career at Elstree.

Valerie tried her luck in Hollywood and starred with *Boris Karloff* in one of the 1930s *"Frankenstein"* movies, *"The Bride of Frankenstein"*, that is a classic horror movie. She told me in the 1990s *"It was just a few weeks work 60 years ago but I still get fan mail and requests for interviews because of it."*

In the 1940s Valerie enjoyed a successful British film career appearing in such distinguished movies as *"Great Expectations"* and *"Kind Hearts and Coronets"* before retiring to enjoy family life. However, she became better known as the loyal wife in the famous 1960s sex scandal involving her husband, *War Minister John Profumo*, a call girl and a Russian spy. It ruined *John's* political career but he later successfully devoted his life to charitable works.

When *Valerie* died in 1998 I was invited to her memorial service and I wrote to *John* offering my condolences and he sent a nice letter back. It shows the more innocent times the 1960s were that it was such a big scandal when you consider what goes on with some of our *MPs* nowadays.

Valerie Hobson John Profumo and Dame Vera Lynn,
[© PW]

More Famous Names from the Past

Norman Wisdom was certainly a one off and long after his film career ended he remained a national treasure. I met *Norman* a couple of times at *Pinewood Studios* at events organised by *Morris Bright* which were always enjoyable occasions. *Norman* was in his 80s then, but still the natural clown. I sometimes held my breath when he would pretend to trip in case he really fell, as we bounce less well as we get older. It was sad that his final years were blighted by senile dementure.

I once asked *Alastair Sim* for an autograph but he very politely declined explaining that he did not believe in such aspects of stardom, which I respected. *George Cole* is another actor quite unlike his wide-boy screen image and more than once he declined my invites to attend showbiz events. He is a very private man and such occasions held no interest for him.

One really brief encounter with an A-list star happened when I at last got round to going to see *"The Mousetrap"* play in London. As I came out after the show I noticed several photographers clicking away in my direction. I modestly thought it can't be me they are interested in so I turned around and a few steps behind me was *Tom Hanks.* I quickly moved aside and departed but I now regret not getting him to sign my programme as a record of the occasion.

I did correspond with a couple of famous authors in the 1970s about film versions of their novels made in Borehamwood.

I asked *Agatha Christie* about the *"Miss Marple"* films *MGM* made in the early 1960s to which she replied *"Margaret Rutherford was a splendid actress but totally miscast in the role and the films bore little resemblance to my books."*

**Dame Margaret
Rutherford.**

[© PW]

Dennis Wheatley, the writer of many supernatural thrillers, told me about the *Hammer Film* versions of his books made at *Elstree*.

He remarked *"The Lost Continent" was a complete mess of my work but "The Devil Rides Out" was a splendid effort. In fact I was very impressed by the actor Charles Gray who played the villain in the film and I wrote him a fan letter c/o Hammer's offices. They returned the unopened envelope to me with written on the outside "Not known at this address", which stunned me."*

I have helped out with a couple of television programmes in my time beyond just being interviewed for them. One was called *"Most Haunted Live"* and they did one show from *Elstree Studios*. I helped brief them on local matters and history and was due to appear on the show, but was dropped for some reason. They had an audience at the studio, but would send the ghost hunters off with a camera crew to other sites and provide a live feedback. Personally I thought it was a load of old rubbish, but it was a very popular show.

The other one was in 1988 when I was engaged by *BBC TV* to be programme consultant on a two-part documentary entitled *"Elstree Britain's Hollywood"*. Budgets as ever were limited so the story of film production in Borehamwood only went up to 1970 to avoid the costs of film clips from more recent hits such as *"Star Wars"* and *"Indiana Jones"*. It was decided that *David Puttnam* would be the on-screen host and he told me *"As a kid living in North London I used to cycle out to Borehamwood and stand outside the studios hoping to spot a star. Later I had a flat in Elstree."*

For the opening sequence we filmed *David* cycling along Shenley Road on a bike borrowed from *"EastEnders"*. There were a number of veterans interviewed including director *Michael Powell* who recalled helping to create the first film union in the 1930s at meetings held at the *Crown Pub* in Shenley Road.

I also remember clambering onto the roof of the now demolished *Gate Studios* next to the Borehamwood Rail Station. I was accompanying the TV crew and a film veteran who had worked there in the 1940s. He related the story of how in those days a junior member of the crew was sent up to the roof with a pair of binoculars and sat in a *'crows nest'* which was linked to the sound stage via a bell. Whenever he saw a train coming in either direction, which were less frequent then, he would judge the distance and then ring the alarm bell so they would stop filming until the train had gone. The problem was that the sound and vibration caused a problem for the film makers, as the stage had originally been built in the silent era.

We only briefly covered the marvellous and unique film history of our town and in subsequent years several companies have contacted me about making further documentaries on the subject, but nothing ever seems to happen. I am afraid budgets seem tighter than ever and the cost of film clips can be prohibitive. It is a great shame, as we are losing more veterans every year and I believe it is a missed opportunity.

The Gate Studios awaiting demolition. I was the last person to conduct filmed interviews on the site. [© PW]

Street Names

From the late 1970s, I was consulted by Hertsmere Council regarding the naming of roads on former Studio sites and I am happy to say my suggestions were accepted.

However, I appreciate that, as only surnames were used, many local residents and visitors alike will know nothing of the characters behind the names of these roads.

When the *Gate Studios* was demolished in Station Road, the Council and the housing developer accepted the following suggested names. The road is called *Whitehall Close* after the original name of the studio opened in 1928. Then we have *Wilding Court* named after 1940s screen heart-throb *Michael Wilding* (1912-1979) who started as an extra at *Elstree Studios* in the 1930s and starred opposite *Anna Neagle* in a series of very popular 1940s movies, before marrying *Elizabeth Taylor*.

Granger Court is named after *Stewart Granger* (1913-1993), who began his career as an extra with *Michael* Wilding at *Elstree* and later married *Jean Simmons*. *Stewart* enjoyed great success in the 1940s at *Gainsborough Studios* in London and then again in the 1950s at *MGM* in Hollywood and Borehamwood.

Odette Court is named after a film made at the *Gate Studios* in 1950. It was based on the real life tale of *Odette Hallowes* (1912-1995), who was born in France, but living in England when the Second World War was on. She bravely volunteered for the S.O.E. and returned to occupied Europe as a spy, but was caught and interned in *Ravensbruck Concentration Camp*. Luckily she survived and was awarded the *George Cross*. I had the pleasure to chat with *Odette* on the phone in the 1980s. A very brave lady.

Odette playing at a London Cinema.
[© PW]

In Furzehill Road, we have *Fairbanks Lodge* named after the famous father and son actors and in Clarendon Road, we have *Neptune Court* recalling the name of the first film studio to open in Borehamwood in 1914 on the site now occupied by the *BBC Elstree Centre.*

The majority of the film-related street names are on the site of the former *Metro Goldwyn Mayer Studios* off Elstree Way, now known as the Studio Estate.

Again, I was happy to suggest the names that were adopted from the 1970s onwards. Some are named after film studios located elsewhere such as *Pinewood, Shepperton, Bray, Ealing, Denham, Danzigers, and Gate* plus *Cygnet,* which was a small studio in Bushey. *Lion Court* represents the famous symbol of *MGM* on all their films.

Individuals who had starred or made films at the various studios in Borehamwood were also recognised. *Herbert Wilcox* (1890-1977) and *Sir Michael Balcon* (1896-1977) were famous film producers in their day. *Herbert* also directed films and was a co-founder of *Elstree Studios.*

Home grown talent, such as *Ray Milland* (1905-1986) who won an Oscar for *"The Lost Weekend"*; *Dame Anna Neagle* (1904-1986) film star and one-time local resident; *Ivor Novello* (1893-1951) famous actor and music composer after whom the music awards are still named; *Leslie Banks* (1890-1952) actor; *James Mason* (1909-1984) superb screen villain and two time Oscar winner; and *Vivien Leigh* (1913-1967), were honoured as was *Charles Laughton* (1899-1962) who was great as *"Captain Bligh"* in the 1930s version of *"Mutiny On The Bounty"*

Vivien Leigh and Charles Laughton play around at the front of Elstree Studios in the 1930s. [© PW]

Vivien Leigh and Sir Laurence Olivier. [© PW]

On the comedy front, we remembered *Joyce Grenfell* (1910-1979), who most people recall from the *"St Trinians"* films; *Tony Hancock* (1924-1968) famous comedy actor of the 1950s and 60s who sadly committed suicide; and *Peter Sellers* (1925-1980) always remembered for the *"Pink Panther"* films, although off screen a troubled and difficult person.

Jack Buchanan (1891-1957) a big name in the 1930s on stage and film and, of course, *Dame Margaret Rutherford* (1892-1972) who made the successful *"Miss Marple"* film series at *MGM* in the 1960s.

Celia Johnson Court was named after stage and screen star *Dame Celia* (1908-1982), best remembered for starring with *Trevor Howard* in the 1940s weepie *"Brief Encounter"*.

John Gregson (1919-1975) starred in several films made in Borehamwood and a 1960s TV series entitled *"Gideons Way'"*

American actors were also included, hence black actor and singer *Paul Robeson* (1898-1976); *Grace Kelly* (1928-1982) who co-starred with *Clark Gable* at *MGM* in *"Mogambo"* before becoming *Her Serene Highness Princess Grace of Monaco.* She was killed in a car crash in 1982.

Then there is *Gary Cooper* (1901-1961) who made his last ever film *"The Naked Edge"* at *Elstree*; *Gene Kelly* (1912-1996) legendary screen dancer; and *Merle Oberon* (1911-1979), a film beauty of the 1930s and 1940s who began her career here.

Merle Oberon. [© PW]

The naming process continues. At the time of writing two new housing estates are being built on land adjacent to the former *MGM* site. Once again I was happy to provide names so we should be seeing *Korda Close* named after *Sir Alexander Korda* (1893-1956) famous film producer long associated with the town.

There will be *Bergman Court* after actress *Ingrid* (1915-1982) who made *"Inn of the Sixth Happiness"*, *"Anastasia"* and *"Murder on the Orient Express"* in the town.

Legendary *Spencer Tracy* (1900-1967) is remembered with *Tracy Court*. Other courts are being named after *Ava Gardner* (1922-1990), *Margaret Lockwood* (1916-1990), and *Sir Alfred Hitchcock* (1899-1980).

Actor *William Holden,* (1918-1981), made several films here, but was a bit of a tragic figure who seemed to have good looks, family, fame, and money, but became an alcoholic. He was found in his penthouse having been dead for several days. The coroner ruled that while drunk he had slipped on a mat and cut his head badly on a bedside table. He had apparently tried to stem the bleeding with hankies but failed to summon help.

Garson Court remembers actress *Greer Garson* (1904-1996) who won the hearts of cinemagoers on both sides of the Atlantic and an Oscar for playing the title role in the classic *"Mrs Miniver"*. Contrary to movie myth, when collecting her award, she did not speak for an hour but just a few minutes.

The other three courts are named after *Sir John Mills* (1908-2005), *Richard Todd* (1919-2009) and *Robert Taylor* (1911-1969). The latter starred in several films made at *MGM* including *"Ivanhoe"* and *"Knights Of The Round Table"*.

I like to think all these people would be very chuffed to know we have remembered them in this way. Who knows they might name a road after me once I kick the bucket – Welsh Way perhaps?

Ava Gardner. [© PW]

Ingrid Bergman and David Kossoff at Elstree.
[© PW]

Signed photo of Danny Kaye who was making
'Peter Pan' at ATV Studios in the 1970s. [© PW]

Signed photo of Kirk Douglas. [© PW]

Signed photo of Joan Crawford
while she was making her last ever film 'Trog'. [© PW]

Signed photo of Lana Turner while she was in the
UK making 'Persecution' in the early 1970s. [© PW]

Metro Goldwyn Mayer British Studios

I will finish my personal memories with recollections of three days over 40 years ago that were a once in a lifetime experience.

The *Metro Goldwyn Mayer British Studios* located in *Elstree Way*, Borehamwood began life as *Amalgamated Studios* in 1936, but the owner defaulted on the mortgage and the builders took control. They sold it to *J. Arthur Rank* who promptly leased it to the government when the Second World War was imminent.

During WW2, the sound stages were used for the manufacture of aircraft parts by *Handley Page.* On at least one occasion, the Studio was hit by a bomb.

In 1944 the Studio was purchased by *MGM.* They also bought the adjacent *Thrift Farm,* creating a site of about 115 acres with 20 acres comprising the buildings and the rest a backlot.

They spent a great deal of money upgrading and modernising the facility and their first film made after the War was *"Edward My Son"* starring *Spencer Tracy* and *Deborah Kerr.*

During the 1950s they made movies with *Clark Gable, Ava Gardner, Robert Taylor, Gene Kelly* and *Elizabeth Taylor* and the Studio became known as the *Rolls Royce* of *UK dream factories*. It also credited the films as produced at *MGM British Studios, Boreham Wood, England* rather than the generic use of *Elstree*. In fact, in one star-studded movie, *"The VIP's"*, they planted an in-joke when *Orson Welles'* character complains that his accountant has got lost in some woods called *Boreham.*

In the 1960s the hits continued with low budget movies such as *"Village Of The Damned"* and *"Quatermass And The Pit"* to big budget efforts like *"2001"*, *"Where Eagles Dare"* and *"The Dirty Dozen"*. In particular I recall the latter due to the night shooting, which involved almighty explosions that were heard throughout the town.

Television also featured with hit series like *"Danger Man"*, *"The Prisoner"* and *"UFO"*, but a full history can wait until I muster the strength for a book about this magnificent studio.

MGM British Studios in the 1940s. [© PW]

View from the MGM Clocktower towards Boreham Wood in the 1940s. [© PW]

Liz Taylor and Robert Taylor filming at MGM in 1949. [© PW]

A young Liz Taylor at MGM. [© PW]

The Ivanhoe Castle under construction. [© PW]

Fight scene on the MGM Castle in the 1950s
Notice the less than medieval goalposts accidentally appearing in the background. [© PW]

The premiere of 'Ivanhoe' at the Empire, Leicester Square. [© PW]

Andrew Keir and Barbara Shelley
celebrating Andrew's birthday on the 'Quatermass and the Pit' set at MGM. [© PW]

Rex Harrison and Jeanne Moreau enjoying a joke as they enter a sound stage at the MGM studios. [© PW]

The legendary Clark Gable out for a stroll in London while filming at MGM in the 1950s. [© PW]

However, by 1970 **MGM** was fast becoming a shadow of its former self with the parent company making big losses in America. **Kirk Kerkorian** was now the company owner and he sent his hatchet man, a guy named **James 'smiling cobra' Aubrey**, over to close the Borehamwood Studio.

It happened fairly quickly and the fate of this state-of-the-art movie-making complex was sealed. It was sold to a property company, so I decided to approach them and ask if I could visit the Studio.

They replied saying they would allow me three days, so on the appointed date I turned up at the gatehouse.

There was just one security man and his vicious-sounding guard dog presiding over the whole site.

He said *"Go where you want mate"* and, with a set of keys, I set off to explore.

I could not believe I had a 115 acre studio all to myself as I first wandered up to the backlot. There I found a street-set used in a number of

productions with the façades of the buildings slowly decaying.

There was a Chinese-looking village with a stream running through it and the remains of the French Chateau featured in the climax of *"The Dirty Dozen"*.

There were various staircases leading to nowhere and a rusting cable car used in *"Where Eagles Dare"*, as well as a number of plaster tombstones used in a **Sammy Davis Jr** comedy.

Then I backtracked to look around the 20 acres of buildings. In a workshop I found plaster moulds of props from *"2001"* and cups of tea half-drunk as if I had boarded the **Mary Celeste**.

I entered the sound stages that seemed gigantic, but now stood empty and dark. I could almost hear **Clark Gable** and **Grace Kelly** rehearsing a scene from *"Mogambo"* or **Liz Taylor** and **Richard Burton** making eyes at each other on the set of *"The VIPs"*. There were so many ghosts inhabiting this forlorn scene, but it is hard to conjure up that feeling in words.

Elstree Confidential

MGM British Studios' headed notepaper

One of the dressing rooms at MGM. [© PW]

Olivia de Havilland undergoing costume tests at MGM, who misspelled her name on the board.

I went up through the dressing rooms that awaited the return of *Ava Gardner* or *Sharon Tate* who would never come.

Then I headed into the makeup department, where, scattered on the floor, were 10x8 inch photographs of stars and guidance notes on how makeup was to be applied.

In another room, I found box files full of production material for countless films. These were later moved to *Elstree Studios* and 19 years later I was asked to list them, as the building in which they were lodged was due to be demolished to make way for Tesco. They were then returned to *MGM* in London, but I later heard this valuable research material was junked to save storage costs! Now I would have kept the lot. In another room I found a pile of film scripts from every film made there and was offered them at £2 each, but 40 years ago I was only earning about £10 a week, so I passed and that hurts now.

The buildings survived a couple more years, whilst planning permission was sorted, and were then demolished to make way for a cold storage plant. The famous White Clocktower and admin. block survived until the mid 1980s, when it too was demolished to make way for a car park. I made efforts to get it listed, backed by our then MP *Cecil Parkinson,* but *English Heritage* decided it was not of significant historical or architectural importance. We even knew of a company willing to buy it and restore it as an up-market art-deco office, but all to no avail.

Sadly, this was before video cameras and even before I had a decent camera, so I was able only to make a meagre recording of this great studio.

Today, with access to video cameras and digital photography, I could have recorded so much that now exists only in my fading memory.

It was a magical experience that these few words cannot really capture.

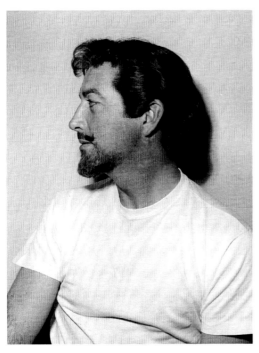
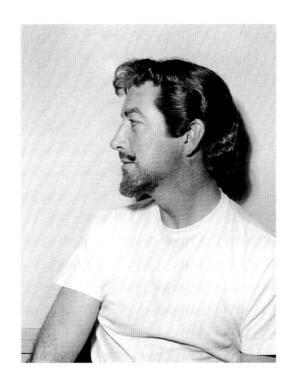
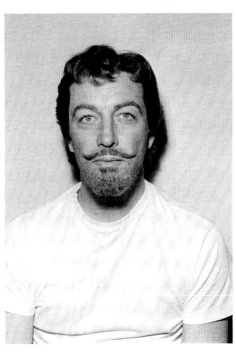

Elizabeth Taylor and Robert Taylor in Ivanhoe

Above:
Makeup shots of Robert Taylor
found scattered on the floor of
the closed MGM Studios. [© PW]

The iconic MGM Clocktower landmark being demolished in the mid 1980s. [© PW]

The Dirty Dozen set on the MGM backlot now occupied by a housing estate. [© PW]

METRO-GOLDWYN-MAYER BRITISH STUDIOS LTD., Boreham Wood, Herts, England.

May 20, 1970

Mr. F. Zinnemann
Timothy Films Limited
128 Mount Street
LONDON.W.1.

Dear Mr. Zinnemann,

As you are probably aware M.G.M. are regretably closing their
Studios at Borehamwood and disposing of the assets. Our
records indicate that you have the following Typewriters in
your possession:-

Adler Manual   Serial number 2306327

Olympia Electric   Serial number 26-12363

If you agree that this is so, perhaps you would either like
to purchase the typewriters or otherwise return them to us as
you choose. Perhaps you could let me know your decision and
if you wish to purchase the machines, how much you are prepared
to offer.

Kind regards,

Yours sincerely,

Norman Swindell

ctors: BENJAMIN MELNIKER (Chairman – U.S.A.) · ARVID L GRIFFEN (Managing Dir. – U.S.A.) · R. B. HUGHES · JACK KING · PAUL MILLS · BASIL SOMNER
phone 01-953-2000 (58 lines)   Telegrams: METROBRIT, BOREHAM WOOD   Telex 22502

Letter to famed Director Fred Zinnemann
from MGM Studios
showing times were tough for the Company

Aerial photo of the MGM Studio Site about 1950. [© EBWM]

Aerial photo of the redeveloped MGM Studio site photographed from a helicopter a few years ago. [© PW]

What they said about Elstree

Presented below are some of the comments that the famous names of motion pictures have said about the Studios of Borehamwood. I used to solicit comments for various anniversaries and these are just a few of them.

Perhaps I should explain at this point why *Elstree* is the name so widely used, whilst all but one of the Studios are or were based in Borehamwood, or Boreham Wood as I called it when I was growing up here. Many think this is something to do with snobbery but that is not correct. You must remember that when the Studios arrived, Borehamwood was basically a farming hamlet clustered around Theobald Street and Shenley Road. Even during the 1930s and early 1940s farmland bordered onto the Studios. It was natural, therefore, that they adopted the name of the better known *Elstree Village* with its similarly named *Railway Station.*

Congratulations on 75 years of film and television production in Borehamwood. To millions of cinemagoers throughout the world *Elstree* means film. We have to thank the Studios there for a wealth of magical entertainment – *Prime Minister Margaret Thatcher* (1989)

I am astonished to find that the Film Studios in Borehamwood were opened the year I was born, a lifetime ago. Please accept my warmest congratulations on such a lengthy persevering production and successful contribution to the film world – *Sir Alec Guinness* (1989)

I have only had the pleasure of shooting one film at *Elstree.* It was stirring to find ourselves working on a stage where so many of Britain's greatest film makers had produced historic pictures. It was also a pleasure to be serviced so efficiently and cheerfully by the workers at *Elstree – Lindsay Anderson* (1989)

I spent some of my best years of my life at Borehamwood working at four of the Studios – *George Cole* (1989)

Elstree and Borehamwood have great memories for me. Firstly, for all the films I made at *ABPC* and also three good years at *ATV* with *Leslie Crowther* in *"My Good Woman"* - *Sylvia Syms* (1989)

Having done all my *"On The Buses"* films at *Elstree Studios* and musical specials at *ATV* I would like to congratulate my good friend *Paul Welsh* for all his dedication and hard work – *Reg Varney* (1989)

I'd like to add my congratulations to those I'm certain you've had on this occasion. It elicited many fond memories having worked there so often – *Charlton Heston* (1989)

I send you my congratulations and wish you much luck for the future – *Sir John Mills* (1989)

I hope another 75 years of distinguished and brilliant film making will follow – *Paul Scofield* (1989)

I always loved working at *Elstree* – just the right size so that you feel you belong and everyone was always so co-operative and friendly - *Glenda Jackson* (1989)

Very bravely done on the campaign. You must all at times felt you were *David* taking the field against *Goliath* and you won. Thank you for keeping one of the best studios open – *George Baker* (1996)

I have many happy memories of working in the studios – *Diana Rigg* (1989)

Elstree and Borehamwood has made a unique contribution to the history of film making. I have personally great affection for and many happy memories of my main place of work for 16 years – *Richard Todd* (1989)

I would just like to send you many congratulations for the past 75 years – Up Elstree! -*Frankie Howerd* (1989)

I have such happy memories of some of my early movies made there and send my continued admiration- *Deborah Kerr* (1989)

My films at Elstree were a highlight of my career- long live *Elstree Studios – Cliff Richard* (1989)

I made several pictures at *MGM* which was well equipped with a friendly and pleasant atmosphere – *Olivia De Havilland* (1997)

I made two pictures at *MGM* not long after the war and it was still being fitted out but the crews were experienced. I enjoyed going for a drink with the lads in the local pubs – *Gene Kelly* (1989)

Without *Elstree* the British cinema would have lost half its history – *Bob Hoskins* (1989)

Elstree Studios and *fish* will always be inextricably linked in my memory. The Studios were extremely comfortable. The fish costume I was wearing at the start of *"The Meaning Of Life"* certainly wasn't. But if you have to play fifth fish with four foot of haddock costume trailing behind you then there is no better place to do it than *Elstree*. I am proud to have been associated in a small but fishy way with the proud tradition that *Elstree* conjures up in the mind of any moviegoer of my generation – *Michael Palin* (1997)

Please remember me to Stage 5. The crews at *Elstree* were the best in the business and it was a joy to work there – *Patrick Macnee* (2011)

I have always enjoyed working at *Elstree* and as you grow older the memories of films I have worked on there grow ever more vivid. I have particularly happy memories of *"Ben Hur"*, *"La Dolce Vita"*, *"Intolerance"* and *"Back To Africa"*. What fun *Gina Lollobrigida* and I had in the canteen. – *John Cleese* (1997)

Elstree Studios has played a very important role in my films. Without the outstanding facilities I would not have been able to make the *"Star Wars"* and *"Indiana Jones"* trilogies. *Elstree Studios* has been vital to filmmakers around the world and is an historical landmark – *George Lucas* (1997)

Elstree Studios has been my home many times in the past 20 years. *George Lucas* had made *"Star Wars"* there and enthused about the spirit and flair, the magic that could be found behind an ordinary suburban high street. *"Indiana Jones"* was born on the sound stages of *Elstree* although conceived somewhere warmer on a beach in Hawaii. When I needed an *English* studio there was no question in my mind where I wanted to be – *Steven Spielberg* (1997)

First Impressions

The *First Impressions* project was a scheme that seemed to take up a fair amount of my time in 2010 and 2011 and is a long overdue public way of celebrating our town's unique film and television heritage. Grants were obtained from Central and Local Government and we embarked on theming the high street and the rail station forecourt with film images, banners, heritage boards, stars in the station forecourt and a giant wall relief depicting a film crew at work. To be honest my input was minimal compared with local resident *Bob Redman* who chaired and drove the project supported by *Hilary Shade*, an officer of *Hertsmere Borough Council*. Others also rallied to the cause to help design and implement the scheme and I must mention *Mike Rollins* who designed the new Plaque boards located in Shenley Road. The hope is to continue this *Film and TV Heritage Trail* and one day have a heritage centre possibly at *Elstree Studios*.

In May 2011 I had the pleasure to host the launch of the first phase with a ceremony, which I felt should be in two sections. One was outdoors at the station forecourt and the other at *Elstree Studios*.

This presented the challenge of how to get the guests backwards and forwards. I thought it would be great to do this in 1960s double-decker buses, as a nod to the *Elstree-made "Summer Holiday"* and the *"On The Buses"* films. *Dean Sullivan* of *Sullivan Buses* rode to the rescue and provided two such buses free of charge. I also asked *Barbara Windsor MBE* if she would unveil the scheme.

You could not have a better people-person for such a task. *Barbara* is delightful and friendly with everyone, whether being asked to pose for photos or sign autographs.

I am also grateful to *Scott,* her charming husband, who helped make things run smoothly.

I must admit it seemed surreal to find myself a passenger on a Routemaster double-decker driving along Shenley Road with *Barbara Windsor* and various people dressed up as characters from *"Star Wars"*, but it was great fun. Those marvellous character actors *Philip Madoc* and *Burt Kwouk* along with director *John Hough* joined us at the station to unveil a Plaque honouring *Peter Sellers* and the *Heritage Trail Board.* The event ran smoothly and proved a great success, but once again that was with the help of our volunteers from *Elstree Screen Heritage* and others who assisted.

Morris Bright and Roger Morris at the First Impressions opening ceremony with Barbara Windsor. [© FI]

Barbara escorted by Darth Vader through a Stormtroopers' Guard of Honour. [© FI]

A First Impression artwork displayed at Elstree and Borehamwood Station. [© EBWM]

Elstree Confidential

Relaxing with Barbara Windsor MBE at the First Impressions launch [© FI]

Elstree Film and Television Screen Heritage Trail Poster. [© FI]

Conclusion

I could repeat many more comments made to me over the decades, but hopefully you get the picture. *Elstree and Borehamwood* has a unique motion picture heritage for us to celebrate. For the past 35 years I have written a weekly column in the *Elstree & Borehamwood Times* and so it is always gratifying when readers of all ages tell me how much they enjoy reading about our Studios and the stars who have worked here.

I am a film historian, without written academic qualifications, but I have lived through and participated in the history about which I have written. I organised the 50th, 60th, 70th and 75th anniversaries of *Elstree Studios*, the 60th anniversary of the *Gate Studio* and the 75th anniversary of the town's first studio. I have met hundreds of actors and visited countless film sets.

I dedicate this book to the memory of my late Mother, Eileen, who was always there to encourage my efforts and who gave me my first film book in the 1960s, which inspired so much of my interest in motion pictures.

I have written this book in just a few weeks and from memory, so my profound apologies to anyone I have forgotten to mention. I know there will be many. It does not reflect on their importance but just my lack of preparation.

The smell of a film studio, the magic of walking onto a sound stage, the kick out of meeting a film star you have admired on screen: I have never taken any of it for granted, but always felt privileged. The 32 years I spent with the Town Council gave me the opportunity, in association with *Elstree Studios,* to organise so many events to celebrate our cinematic past.

I must thank *Keith Clement,* one-time head of *BBC Elstree Centre,* for his support and agreeing to several Open Days at that Studio. I owe a debt of gratitude to the late *Andrew Mitchell* MBE, Managing Director of *Elstree Studios,* for indulging and financing my efforts to organise anniversary events. A special thanks to *Ian Marshall* and *Mike Crisp* for creating the *BBC Elstree Band* who played such excellent music at many of these events and to *John Herron,* who provided films for us to show, free of charge.

Many of us may feel the night closing in as we grow older, but I am not yet ready for the final curtain! So that's it folks and thank you for sharing my memories. If you have stayed the course and are still reading, that's almost it for now.

I could tell you about attending the launch of *"The Muppet Show"* at *ATV* in the 1970s, ending up on stage with *Paul Daniels* or seeing *Christopher Reeve* as *"Superman"* suspended over *Shenley Road*. I could recall *Michael Jackson's* secret visit to *Elstree Studios* or the filming of the *"Bohemian Rhapsody"* video with *Queen*. Tales of *Stanley Kubrick* and *Jack Nicholson* filming *"The Shining"* spring to mind, along with quite a few other memories, but they must wait for another time.

Paul Welsh MBE

More Photos from my Album

Gregory Peck and family arriving in England where he was to make the film "Hornblower" at Elstree. Tragically his young son Johnathan in the photo (1944-1975) later killed himself with a gun. [© PW].

Bryan Forbes, on his appointment as Head of Elstree Studios in 1969, is joined by stars including Roger Moore and Lionel Jeffries and EMI boss Bernard Delfont. [© PW]

Nanette Newman, Neville Reid, Bryan Forbes and PW. [© PW]

Ingrid Pitt visiting Elstree Studios in the 1990s. [© PW]

The audience at the old Venue for a BBC Elstree Band concert. [© PW]

Mike Crisp, Helen Cherry and PW judging local Camcorder Club competition. [© PW]

Berrnard Delfont with his brother Lew Grade

I was laughing at one of Simon's stories with singer Rob Dodkin (left) and Liam Doran in the background.
[© KM]

Patrick Macnee and Diana Rigg greeting visitors to the set of the Avengers at Elstree in the 1960s. [© PW]

Appropriate adults on a visit to the Police Riot-Control Training Centre. [© PW]

Set designer Keith Harris, Head of the BBC Elstree Centre, Keith Clement, Mayor Eileen Stanley and myself on the set of EastEnders just when it was about to debut in about 1985. [© PW]

Sarah Lawson, Patrick Allen, Philip Madoc and myself at 1990s Elstree Film Evening. [© PW]

Philip Madoc. [© CM]

American film students from the University of Miami visiting Elstree Studios in the 1990s. [© PW]

Brian Johnston meets the Elstree Studios manager, John Skinner, on a 'Down your Way' BBC Radio visit I helped organise.[© PW]

Elstree Confidential

My winning 5 a side team sponsored by Elstree Studios. [© PW]

Being an ace batsman the Elstree Cricket Club fielders were taking no chances. [© PW]

The then Dr Who, Peter Davison, Brian Burton and myself 30 years ago. [© PW]

Jack Buchanan and his wife. 1950s [© PW]

Director Stanley Donen celebrates the end of filming 'Indiscreet' at Elstree
with its stars Cary Grant and Ingrid Bergman. [© PW]

Elstree contract star John Fraser who had to hide being gay in the 1950s
when such things could destroy a young leading man's career. [© PW]

Darth Vader with Elstree Film Veteran, Ron Punter

EastEnders' star Ricky Groves and Mayor Ernie Butler present the winning trophy
on families day to my team of Nick, Mike, David, Davide, Matt, Dan and Rick. [© PW]

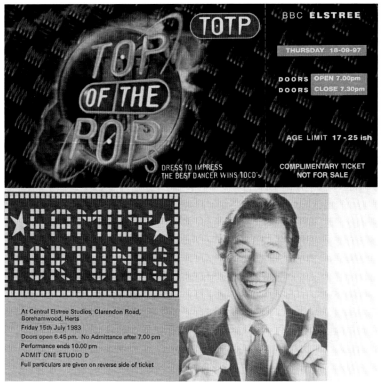

A selection of tickets from the countless TV shows I have watched being recorded

Index - People

Peter Duncan	24	Ava Gardner	37,152	Rita Hayworth	18,101
John East	6		153,155	Paul Henreid	145
Shirley Eaton	122		162	Nicky Henson	122
EBW Museum	2	Greer Garson	152	Katherine Hepburn	16
Britt Ekland	19	William Gaunt	122	John Herron	92,172
Paul Eddington	36	Eunice Gayson	134	Charlton Heston	57,167
Noel Edmonds	56	HM King George V	89	Jean Heywood	42
Mark Eden	48	HM King George VI	90	Martin Heywood	41
Prince of Edward VIII Wales	90	George Gibbs	77	Harry Hill	100
		Guy Gibson	33	Jim Hill	73,91
Jimmy Edwards	56	Dorothy Gish	107	Fraser Hines	122
Peter Egan	122	Lilian Gish	107	Thora Hird	117,122
HM Queen Elizabeth The Queen Mother	90	Julian Glover	117	Sir Alfred Hitchcock	6,7,8
		Johnny Goodman	58,134		72,107
Vera Ellen	13	Marius Goring	120,122		115,143
James Ellis	118,122	Frank Gorschin	39		144,152
Jenny Ellis	64	Walter Gotell	120,122	Valerie Hobson	146
Sylvia Ellwood	68	Gill Gowing	73	Glen Hoddle	24
Elstree Youth Theatre	63	Lord Lew Grade	1178119	William Holden	50,152
			122,139	Bob Hope	14
Lee Evans	37		177	Bob Hoskins	168
Douglas Fairbanks	6,21,22,	Sean Graham	38,86	John Hough	58,77
	23,36,56		99		134,169
	117,121	Stewart Granger	61,149	Trevor Howard	35,46
	127,150	Cary Grant	6,37		82,94
Adam Faith	117,120		145,183		151179
Festival Queens	43	Leslie Grantham	22	Frankie Howerd	46,168
		Charles Gray	148	Geoffrey Hughes	122
Shirley Ann Field	122	Dulcie Gray	117,121	Nerys Hughes	122
Ralph Fiennes	104,127	Jimmy Greaves	56	Alan Hume	134
	128	Hughie Green	120,122	Benita Hume	111
Peter Finch	17	Teddy Green	113	Gareth Hunt	121,122
Susan Finlay	64,84	Ron Greenwood	29	Tab Hunter	92
First Impressions	2,169,	John Gregson	151	Wilfred Hyde White	94
	190,171	Joyce Grenfell	151	Tommy Ibbetson	127
Peter Firth	46	Richard Griffiths	117	John Inman	49,118
Carrie Fisher	97	Joe Grossman	9,90	Glenda Jackson	167
Bud Flannagan	6	Richard Grove	73	Michael Jackson	172
Errol Flynn	13,35,	Ricky Groves	184	Sir Peter Jackson	56
	58,116	John Grover	134	Sid James	51
	117,128	Sir Alec Guinness	97,167	Derek Jameson	56
Bryan Forbes	45,117	Tony Hadley	100	Lionel Jeffries	174
	120,130	Garrick Hagon	122	Stratford Johns	117,122
	174,175	Odette Hallowes	149	Celia Johnson	151
Harrison Ford	7,33	Mark Hamill	24,97	Richard Johnson	19,45
	71,97	Tony Hancock	151	Van Johnson	23
John Ford	49	Tom Hanks	147	Brian Johnston	177
George Formby	6	Keith Harris	179	Al Jolson	17
Steve Forrest	136	Richard Harris	33	Jack Jones	39
Barry Foster	122	Norman Harrison	82	Peter Jones	118,122
Christopher Fountain	37	Nick Harrison	73	Tom Jones	38
Derek Fowlds	122	Rex Harrison	159	Yootha Joyce	139
Michael J Fox	16	Ray Harryhausen	122	Boris Karloff	15,48
Freddie Francis	58,122	Diane Hart	13		49,117
	125	Eva Hart	22,77		146
Graeme Franklin	118		118,119	Danny Kaye	154
William Franklyn	122	Laurence Harvey	33	Buster Keaton	7,18
Bill Fraser	37	Sir Nigel Hawthorne	26,117	Kevin Keegan	29
John Fraser	183		120	Andrew Keir	159
Liz Fraser	26,120	Steve Hay	68	Madeline Kellock	134
	122,132	Will Hay	43,124	Barbara Kelly	117
Emma Freud	56	Stirling Hayden	44,139	Gene Kelly	59,151
Clark Gable	7,37	Melvyn Hayes	122		155,168
	128,151				
	155,160				

Leon Reefe 120
Christopher Reeve 172
Neville Reid 87,105
124,176
Debbie Reynolds 16,97
Sir Tim Rice 113
Sir Cliff Richard 113,114
130,168
Diana Rigg DBE 168,178
Wolf Rilla 111
Shane Ritchie 51
Graham Rix 24
Pam Roach 43
Cliff Robertson 23
Paul Robeson 151
Ginger Rogers 23,59
107
Roy Rogers 107
Mike Rollins 169
Caesar Romero 13
Mickey Rooney 37
Norman Rossington 122
Leonard Rossiter 139
Bill Ruck 56
Jane Russell 102
Margaret Rutherford 147,151
DBE
Andrew Sachs 122
Sir Sydney Samuelson 73,84
118,120
125
George Sanders 111
Jonathan Sands 2,4
Paul Sattin 72
Max Schmeling 144
Paul Scofield 167
Doug Scott 58
Janette Scott 117,122
Peter Sellers 45,50
109,151
Julian Senior 58
George Sewell 120,122
Hilary Shade 169
Barbara Shelley 111,132
159
Ben Shepherd 41,42
Dinah Sheridan 94,143
Carmen Silvera 109
Alastair Sim 147
Jean Simmons 149
Ben Simon 64,84
Frank Sinatra 35,109
Sir Donald Sinden 36,37
John Skinner 177
Chris Smith 85
Sir C Aubrey Smith 82
Ivan Sopher 68
David Soul 38
Spandau 100
Ballet

Steven Spielberg 7,68
69,71
72,97
168
Rosemary Squires 118
Pam St Clement 131
Bryan Stanley 87,89
Eileen Stanley 83,179
Marcia Stanton 134
Graham Stark 117,122
Anthony Steel 51
James Stewart 49
Rod Stewart 99
John Stride 46
Allan Stronach 63
Milton Subotsky 19
Mollie Sugden 122,123
Dean Sullivan 47,169
Jeremy Summers 131,134
Eric Sykes 117,122
Sylvia Syms 7,125,
132,167
Take That 93
Gillian Taylforth 22
Christopher Tarrant 37
Sharon Tate 18,162
Eileen Tatler 140
David Taylor 4
Elizabeth Taylor 58,102
107,125
149,155
156,157
163
Robert Taylor 152,155
156,163
Shaw Taylor 51
Stanley Taylor 73
Lady Thatcher 167,96
Margaret
The Ink Spots 39
HM Queen 100
Elizabeth
Terry -Thomas 47
Christopher Timothy 120,122
Ann Todd 122
Richard Todd 6,13
33,34
152,168
Torvill and 37
Dean
Spencer Tracy 16,152
155
Tommy Trinder 51
Lana Turner 101,154
Dorothy Tutin 122
Anthony Valentine 19,120
122
Sue Valentine 120
Rudolph Valentino 17
Reg Varney 48,167
Frankie Vaughan 46
Richard Vernon 117
Robert Wagner 23
Ralph Waite 16

George & Walker 71,73
Billy
Zena Walker 92
Bradley Walsh 37
Barbara Walters 91
Simon Ward 46
Jack Warner 46,128
95
Dennis Waterman 39,40
Peter Waterman 123,133
OBE
Jack Watling 120,122
John Wayne 31,32
Weintraub 68
Bill Welsh 10
Eileen Welsh 84,172
Orson Welles 155
John West 133
Mae West 100,101
Wet Wet Wet 93
Dennis Wheatley 148
Leonard Whiting 122
Julie Wicks 87
Richard Widmark 49
Elizabeth Wilcox 127
Herbert Wilcox 107,116
141,150
John Wilcox 127
Jack Wild 120,122
Michael Wilding 116,148
Esther Williams 23
Frank Williams 118,120
122
Jan Williams 134
Robbie Williams 93
Ronan Willson 77
Barbara Windsor 32,45
114,131
169,170
171
Wings 64
Michael Winner 82
Kate Winslet 99
Dale Winton 131
Norman Wisdom 147
Ernie Wise 118,122
Edward Woodward 139
Peter Wyngarde 38
Dana Wynter 54
Michael York 12
Danny Young 41
Freddie Young 58,122
125
Gig Young 111
Jimmy Young 56
Robert Young 107
Terence Young 115
Lady Yule 6
Fred Zinnemann 11,58
165

Index - Productions